EVA COO

Murderess

by

Niles Eggleston

North Country Books
Utica, New York

Eva Coo
Murderess

Cover Art by John Mahaffy

ISBN 0-925168-60-2

Second Printing 2002

NORTH COUNTRY BOOKS, INC.
311 Turner Street
Utica, New York 13501

DEDICATION

I was attending high school in Milford, New York, less than eight miles northwest of the murder site and eight miles south of the trial site, during the time that the Eva Coo affair was unfolding. It was fifty-four years later when, in 1988, Debbie Velasco brought to my attention a notebook full of dated newspaper clippings that covered the Coo murder case. She had received them from her mother, Jane Luchessi, who in turn had inherited them upon the death of her cousin, Nellie Bugbee.

Nellie had been principal of the school on Chestnut Street in Oneonta, New York during her later years, a teacher previously, and an organized collector all of her life.

This fascinating material encouraged me to write an article about the Coo case and it was published in a national magazine. Suddenly, I was hearing from a lot of people with a lot of additional material. It became apparent that Eva Coo had by no means been forgotten.

It also became apparent that while some of her exploits had been narrated in four books, several radio shows, on television, and in countless magazines and newspapers all over the world, still much had been left untold about the murder and nothing had been written about the aftermath.

During the next several years, ferreting out these facts became my obsession. Old accounts were reviewed, documents examined, and scores of people who personally knew Eva were interviewed.

Nellie Bugbee, it was your clippings that started me on this crusade. It is to your memory that I dedicate this book.

ACKNOWLEDGMENTS

I wish to thank the following people for the information or artifacts they supplied and to apologize to any who have inadvertently been overlooked.

Helen Ackler, Lena Anderson, Louise Armstrong, Les Arnold, Walter Beach, Jr., Shirley Bliss, Dorothy Bostwick, Janet Buell, Frances Butler, Marjorie Cahoon, Earl Carr, Norman Carr, Jack and Mabel Chase, Elsie Clough, Alfred and Virginia Compton, Marilou Curtin, Bob Dart, Georgia Decker, Lois V. Denson, Wayne Dolling, Tony Drago, Ted Feury, Dorothy Scott Fielder, Richard Fink, Al Fitzelle, Beverly Graves, Betty Gilbert, Lynne Green, Jr., Ethel Groat and Neil Gumaer.

Wilbur Hansen, Martha Hotaling, Joan Zindle Howard, Lucy Zindle Ireland, Nelson Irons, Heather Kencelik, Anson Knapp, Sr., Charlotte Koniuto, Dorothy LaSalle, Jenny Lane, Morris Liedkie, Gloria Madero, Ed Martin, Lavonia Miller, Jack Mitchell, Joe Mitchell, Peter Molinari, Tony Nilo, Nancy Norton, Leo Patrick Norton, Charles Osborn, Betty Rowley Page, Lucille and Jess Palmatier, Jacob Peake, Frank Pearsall, Florence Porter, Helen and Emma Porteus and Ruby Cronkite Powell.

William Richards, Alton Riddell, Bob Riddell, Florence Ross, Donald Salisbury, Arlene Schmitt, Mary Scott, Edna Seeley, Ann Shepard, Millie Shepard, Floyd Stark, Bob Storm, George Tillapaugh, Marjorie Tillapaugh, Debbie Velasco, Floris Vroman, William Warnken, Jr., Dick Weir, Charles Wightman, Roberta Williams, Deane Winsor, Mrs. Richard Wood, Gary Woodrow and Alice Yager.

A special thank you also to Wendell Tripp of Cooperstown for his invaluable advice in preparing the manuscript.

—*Niles Eggleston*

iv

CONTENTS

INTRODUCTION

One of the most unusual murders of the century occurred in a rural, nearly crime-free township in upstate New York in 1934. The following account is a true story.

Untold thousands of cases of homicides where people have been shot, bludgeoned, carved up, poisoned, suffocated, drowned and mutilated, yes even run down by autos, have occurred since then and still most of these crimes have been forgotten. Yet, after sixty-some years, the Eva Coo case remains a well-remembered episode.

Why? This story certainly is not a "Who Done It." After all, the murderess was quickly apprehended and there remains little doubt about her guilt. Rather it's a story about a woman who lived high in "Sin City" during the roaring twenties, yet was relegated to utter poverty during the Great Depression of the thirties, and her evil plan to remedy her dilemma.

It's the story of a doting mother, dedicating her life to sheltering her child and yet, unwittingly, throwing him into the lion's cage upon her death.

It's the story of that lioness who had almost supernatural control over others and yet who eventually lost complete control over her own destiny and became a pawn for the enrichment of others.

This is the story of greed and corruption by association, in which friend and foe alike became entangled in a web of their own making, a web from which they could never completely extricate themselves.

This is a story of how an event gained such national prominence that those involved both in her defense and prosecution were drawn into their own private battle of egos, while Eva sat in the death house, temporarily forgotten by everyone except the executioner.

This is a story of how little control man has over his own destiny; a story of how the best laid plans of mice, men and Coos can go awry simply by incredibly bad luck and circumstances beyond human control.

This is a story in an era before the phrase "civil rights" was known . . . a period when the law and the police who enforced it believed that the end justified the means. It was an era when the state was too civilized to burn witches bound to a stake but would not hesitate, after a speedy trial, to burn a woman, witch or not, strapped to a chair.

Last but by no means least, this is a story of a condemned woman's revenge . . . a story of dead reputations and dead bodies, all the direct result of Eva's trial.

These are only the most obvious of many reasons why the Eva Coo case remains one of the classics in the annals of crime.

As for the truth, the event was such a sensation at the time that most of the documents have been preserved. The Otsego County Clerk's office has the complete transcript from the trial . . . all 2,268 pages of it. The New York Historical Association has the defense attorney's voluminous files. The original coroner's inquest and countless other documents are in private collections.

Many scrapbooks containing newspaper clippings have been preserved. In matters of trivia accounts differ, but it is possible to recognize the most accurate journalists by comparing their accounts with known facts. Furthermore, if one picks up enough pieces of background material, the correct ones fall into place to create the most likely scenario.

Gone are most of the people who knew the participants, so some questions will never be answered. On the other hand, in the matter of self-preservation, correspondents then were aware of some facts they dared not reveal. Now they can be told. Even more important, we now can see the case in a historic perspective, an advantage not available at the time the events were unfolding.

So, on balance, a far more accurate account can now be told than was possible in the mid-1930's.

CAST OF CHARACTERS

Ames, Earl: Insurance agent who suspected foul play

Brady, Owen P.: Otsego County Deputy Sheriff

Byard, James J., Jr.: With Holmes, was Coo's first attorney

Cadwell, W.E.: Trooper who found the body

Campbell, Edwin R.: Attorney who wrote Wright's will

Carpenter, Harold D.: Justice of Peace who arranged Coo and Clift

Clift, Martha: Co-conspiritor who drove the death car

Coo, Bill: Eva Coo's former husband

Coo, Eva: Planned and participated in the crime

Cross, Henry: Policeman who took the mallet home

Currie, Mrs. Margaret: Eva's mother

Elliott, Robert: Executioner

Ferling, Flen: Lawes' secretary

Fink, Ben: Iva Fink's husband

Fink, Iva: Owner of the Scott farm murder site

Grant, Donald: Prosecuting attorney

Getman, Dr. Norman: Coroner who called death a homocide

Greenough, Dr. James: Performed autopsy

Gunther, "Gunny": Newspaper reporter

Hamm, Charles: Sold Woodbine Inn to Coo; later bought it back

Hanover, Edna: Friend of Eva

Heath, Riley H.: Judge who presided over Grand Jury and trial

Holmes, Everett: With Byard was Coo's first attorney

Hunt, Ben: Clara Hunt's husband

Hunt, Clara: Friend of the Finks

Knapp, Kenneth: Trooper who took evidence, some illegal

Kobler, John: Newspaper man who posed as a secretary

Lawes, Lewis E.: Warden at Sing Sing

Learned, A. Milton: The *Oneonta Daily Star's* city editor

Lehman, Herbert H.: Governor of New York

Loucks, Jesse: Coo's former boyfriend

Maynard, Ernest: Trooper who took evidence, some illegal

Meyers, Clara: Eva's neighbor

Mitchell, George: Otsego County sherriff

Nabinger, Harry: Eva's live-in boyfriend

Palmer, Fred: Meyer's hired hand

Peak, Morris: Owner of death car

Scarnici, Leonard: Electrocuted same day as Coo

Shumway, Gladys: Friend of Clift and Coo

Slade, Maxwell & David: Coo's last attorneys

Stanley, Arthur: Changed date on tombstone

Tennant, Clermont G: Clift's attorney

Thayer, Dr. Walter N., Jr.: New York State Commissioner of Correction

Tillapaugh, Reva: Mortician who buried Wright

Warner, Mary: Claimed a person impersonating Lehman promised pardon

Winsor, Dr. E.C.: Acting coroner called death accidental

Wright, Harry: Coo's handyman and the victim

Wright, Hattriet*: Harry Wright's mother.

Zindle, Harry: Lived near Scott farm

Zindle, Lucy: Harry Zindle's wife

---

* Spelled Hattriet Wright on her tombstone (both first and last engravings), but spelled Harriet on Harry Wright's death certificate. Births were not recorded at the time of her birth in 1858.

Prologue

On June 27, 1935, every radio in east-central New York and many of them nationwide were tuned in, not to enjoy the Cliquot Club Eskimos or the Lux Radio Theater but rather to hear the latest news out of Ossining's Sing Sing Prison. It was the night when Eva Coo was scheduled to be electrocuted.

In the barrooms on Oneonta's Broad Street, patrons stared at their beer or simply sat stone-faced in silence. Some hoped, some feared, that Governor Herbert H. Lehman would step in at the last minute with a stay of execution that would lead to a change in her sentence to life imprisonment, or perhaps even a pardon.

The few prostitutes who had not been driven from the city by the depression were morose, pensive and simply off duty. It made no difference; the johns were not in the mood either.

Up in the big Victorian homes that looked down on the smokey city, prominent business men and politicians sat dutifully beside their wives and children.

Outside of town, in Noble's restaurant, Dorothy Kilgallen was treating Harry Nabinger to a night on the town. Dorothy's motive was to get yet another sensational news story; Harry's was to drown all thoughts of the incriminating evidence he had provided the prosecution at his live-in girlfriend's trial.

Out on the many farms in the countryside, men and women of virtue waited to hear whether or not an evil woman had received her just desserts; and all over the United States and in several foreign countries, the curious simply did not want to miss the final chapter in a drama that they had seen unfold in their daily papers.

Shortly after ten o'clock, listeners in the northeast heard the announcer on radio station WGY Schenectady break into the regular programming to say that Eva Coo had drawn her last breath at 10:02 p.m.

In the seamy part of town, "down and outers" as well as practitioners of the world's oldest profession were not ashamed to shed a tear when the news arrived. Up on the hill, men of means probably embraced their wives, while heaving sighs of relief in the knowledge that past indiscretions would never come to their wives' attention. Out in the hinterlands, the multitudes thanked God that the state still believed that the wages of sin should be death. Harry Nabinger was just too drunk to care.

But did she receive justice? If a person is caught with a smoking gun, has a motive, and a corpse is nearby, he or she is very likely to be a murderer. So it can be argued that justice was served.

Even Warden Lewis E. Lawes never said that she was not guilty, but he fought for her life, saying that she had received "a raw deal." Yet, some wag might comment that Eva, a woman of the world, should have known that when she moved into a railroad town, she might have expected to be railroaded.

During the prosperity of the roaring '20's, she had prospered in a profession that brought rich and poor into the flesh pots where a few uptown men mixed with railroad men and roustabouts in quest of bootleg booze and loose women. There was talk on the street that she should have known better than to threaten, through prison bars, to speak the last word in her "kiss and tell" experiences, as a bargaining chip to gain her freedom. Whether or not that threat had returned to haunt her is pure conjecture. Yet the fact cannot be disputed that in spite of many incidents that would today be grounds for a new trial if not outright dismissal, she was denied an appeal; Robert Elliott pulled the switch that extinguished her life less than a year after her trial began.

If, given the benefit of history, you second-guess the judge and jury, and find the penalty too severe, consider the fate of most of the people with whom she came in contact. From within her grave, this crafty old fox could not have thought up a more diabolical means of destroying her enemies. Yet, had it not been for her own incredibly bad luck, it is likely that Harry Wright would have received a quiet burial, Eva would have lived out her days in obscurity, and her tormentors been spared. But, Lady Luck ran amok. No one was spared.

So, let's go back to another era and review an unusual murder, followed by the most bizarre and incredible chain of events to ever have followed a crime in the annals of history.

PART ONE

WILL THE REAL EVA PLEASE STEP FORWARD?

Eva Coo. It's a simple name, a melodious name, a soothing name. It brings to mind the dove of peace cooing a love song to it's mate. When one adds the name by which she was most frequently called, "Little Eva," the heroine of Uncle Tom's Cabin emerges. If her name implies that she was a simple country girl, she was surely misnamed. A more complex, more complicated personality was never created.

Bald men are often nicknamed "Curly" so it should not be surprising that 5-foot 7-inch tall, 170-pound Mrs. Coo was called "Little Eva." She could be described as solid, yes, even muscular; correspondents called her "the buxom blonde."

In her business it was necessary to be friendly, exuberant and cheerful. To fun loving Eva, that came naturally. Her clients sometimes became rowdy and when that happened, her eyes, hard and cold as steel, would convey the message that she was in charge. Even though she occasionally employed a bouncer, she never really needed one because she was ready, willing, and able to handle the job herself.

Many locals didn't know her personally but had heard of her reputation. When they went to court, they expected to see a tough, middle-aged bootlegger. The tabloids, on the other hand. were billing her as "the blonde siren," "the blonde roadhouse hostess," and "Good Time Eva."

When first arraigned, unkempt, tired and defiant, she certainly did fit the first characterization, but after her lawyers arranged for her to wear attractive clothing, jewelry, makeup, and showed her how to listen to testimony with dignity and a look of ease, she definitely took on the siren's role.

Everyone who saw Eva Coo walk down the street recognized the same body. However, each saw a different side of her complex personality. Here is what a few people thought she was like . . . observations picked from hundreds of quotes from those who thought they knew her.

Her neighbors, after there was no question in their minds but that she had killed a man for profit, stood in shock. From her past, G.M. Evans, her neighbor when she was a newlywed in Calgary, remembered her as "the best neighbor in the world. She was always willing to share whatever she had with one and all."

Her next-door neighbors at the time of the murder were both forced to testify that she asked them to alibi for her. Even so, Fred Palmer recalled, "Coo always treated everyone well," and Clara Meyers said, "Eva was kind to her neighbors."

Dorothy Kilgallen called her "free and easy, an inveterate liar and generous to a fault," as well as "a diabolically clever woman." She wrote a whole column of hate letters from women who claimed Eva had led their husbands down the primrose path to ruin.

Another correspondent called her "loud, profane, lusty, yet generous to a fault," and added that she was "a strange, weird, wild woman."

One called her "a conscienceless vampire who led men down a hard drinking trail to their doom."

In Oneonta she had a reputation of being a paradoxical character who delighted in fleecing the suckers and befriending the outcasts. Just how Oneonta's self appointed Robin Hood could continue to attract the most prominent people in the area to her door is odd indeed, but she did. As Charles Hamm commented, "Big hearted, she took their money and let them have fun—politicians, policemen, doctors, lawyers."

As one can see, different laymen saw a different woman. Yet it is documented that every one of these people was right. She was all of these things and more.

But what was the evaluation of William E. Benton, an eminent New York psychiatrist? He said, "The two sides of her face and nature are so different that we know she is a female Dr. Jekyll and Mr. Hyde. She is probably a very convincing sales person because of her ability to present the good side of any proposition while she deftly covers the defects. She is literally and figuratively a very colorful and romantic personality, despite her sadistic tendencies."

This author (who has interviewed many people who personally knew Eva) would amend Dr. Benton's analysis. The dividing line clearly was not "the two sides of her face" but the two sides of the door that led into her establishment. Those who saw her outside knew a kindly, neighborly, down-to-earth Dr. Jekyll; those who saw her inside knew a wild, crafty "Broadway Lil" masking a treacherous Mr. Hyde.

Perhaps the most interesting and surely the most controversial analysis is in Wenzell Brown's book, *Women of Evil*, published shortly after Eva's death. It deals with modern women who " . . . in another age would have been burned at the stake as witches." Ten pages are devoted to Eva Coo.

When he refers to "the strange revelries and nightly bacchanals" and "weird exhibitions" that went on in her Oneonta speakeasy, one can dismiss it as pure "hogwash," unconfirmed by any other source.

He says that Eva claimed "she was protected by the devil and her little black book," but Eva knew that the little black book was sufficient without the devil's help. What's more, if she was a devil worshiper, he showed his thanks for her adoration by shooting her down with a double barreled whammy gun. After all, she could have pulled it all off except for the incredibly bad luck she had on not just one but two different days!!

However, if we define a witch as someone with the magnetism to draw and control others, you will see this done at its best by Eva. Forget poor Harry Wright with his brain marinated in alcohol, but consider Clift, Shumway and Nabinger, people of average intelligence conspiring in a plot to kill their friend for insurance when they knew that Eva had insurance on each of their own lives!!

Not many of us believe in voodoo. It's foolish to think that any human can cast a spell on another. When one antagonist bites the dust, chalk it up to pure coincidence . . . but when three of them are zapped? Well, keep an open mind until you hear the whole story.

THE TWENTIES ROAR INTO ONEONTA

Oneonta, located in rural Otsego County in upstate New York, sparkles like a jewel within an ever changing setting. The surrounding mountains are clothed in soft emerald green as they herald the birth of spring. The panorama becomes more subdued with richer colors as the warm summer sunbathes the landscape, slowly transforming into a carnival of brilliant orange, scarlet and yellow hues when autumn arrives. As the leaves fall, the glory of naked silver maples interspersed with patches of green conifers and golden larch shines over the sleeping hills. Soon the whole setting is blanketed by snow until the wakening of yet another spring.

Billing itself as "The City of the Hills," this quiet, clean college town has little crime, no slums, and no smokestack industries. This is in sharp contrast to Oneonta during the days of our story.

After World War II, government regulations, outmoded union rules, unfair competition and mismanagement combined to erode the strength of the once mighty Delaware & Hudson Railroad. Bankruptcies followed. At one point it appeared that the line might even be abandoned. This catastrophe was avoided, when in 1991, the D&H was purchased by the Canadian Pacific.

Most of the few trains that now use the tracks are bound for Albany or Binghamton and the engineers do no more than sound a lonely salute as they rush by Oneonta. Gone are the repair shops and roundhouse and with them the jobs that made Oneonta a railroad town bar none.

America concluded "the war to end all wars" in the 1910's; had a big party to celebrate in the 1920's and a hellova hangover in the 1930's. Eva came to town in the turbulent twenties so our interest now is in what she found at that time.

In the 1920's, Oneonta was a flourishing small city located within a vast area of rural poverty. Farmers had no more in common with city folks than did pre-Civil War plantation owners in the south have with the industrialists of the north. The farmer's depression had started soon after the close of World War I, and these people labored in the fields from sunup to sundown just to stay alive. There were no "flappers" on the farms, no dancing to the Charleston in the Grange Halls.

In sharp contrast, Oneonta was a boom town—a prosperous railroad town—a wealthy town that joined in the revelry of the twenties with a vengeance. Yes, in some ways it fell into step with other urban areas; yet in many ways it was uniquely different. First, for the similarities.

The "roaring twenties" were a celebration and a protest. That sounds like a paradox and so it was because the period itself was a paradox. World War I had ended and that called for a celebration; prohibition had begun and that called for a protest. The two contradictory forces were welded to create the zaniest, the wackiest ten years in our history.

Ed Moore, Oneonta's leading historian, describes them as "the roaring twenties, the Jazz Age, the time of flaming youth, the whoopee years, the lawless decade, the era of wonderful nonsense." It was the raucous period when "flappers" wearing cloche hats, knee length skirts, boyish bobbed hair, and stockings rolled down to their knees danced to the feverish beat of the Charleston.

Women were emancipated and openly participated with men in the vices of sex, booze and smoking. Men wore raccoon coats with a flask or two tucked in every pocket. Women wore fur over their short dresses and that was about all, for as Dorothy Parker commended, "Brevity is the soul of lingerie."

Bootlegging was an accepted and prosperous occupation. Speakeasies dispensed their wares under the protection of politicians and the police themselves. Breaking what many perceived to be an unjust law made it easier to break others.

Big time gangsters like Al Capone, "Dutch" Schultz and "Legs" Diamond received better press than Presidents Harding, Coolidge or Hoover while outlaws like Bonnie and Clyde Barrow, Ma Barker, and John Dillinger became folk heroes. (Until he was "wiped out" with a hail of bullets, the New York City mobster, "Legs" Diamond, had connections in Oneonta and had often visited there.)

Yet some extremes were rejected. The Ku-Klux-Klan established a local chapter around 1924. They ignited a few fiery crosses, but mostly caused public outrage. Three attempts at parading the streets in Oneonta were aborted and by the end of the decade the group was disbanded, never to be heard from again.

While Oneonta's participation in the partying followed the nation's norm, the city also had a unique personality of it's own. Think of Oneonta in the 20's as a three layer cake. Using that analogy, the bottom layer was hard and somewhat scorched; the top, rather ordinary; and sandwiched in between, a rich—yes, very rich filling.

It's railroad yards had the largest roundhouse in the world. The complex employed over 2,000 men. Many more maintained the tracks and moved a stream of trains over them. With the exception of the war years, railroads were enjoying their most profitable period ever. Those who worked on them were generously compensated, at least compared to the prevailing wages in the rural countryside.

On River Street, near the rail yards, lived workmen, many of them second or third generation Italian-Americans whose fathers or grandfathers had, with calloused hands, laid the rails in the 1860's. This new generation worked in the rail yards, freight station and repair shops.

The depot was in the nearby Broad and Market Street area. That was where restaurants, flop houses, speakeasies, pool halls and brothels welcomed the workmen's pay checks.

A cavalcade of steam locomotives, some going through pulling long strings of cars laden with anthracite from the coal fields of Pennsylvania, others switching in the yards, belched clouds of smoke and steam that formed a cloud, sealing off the seedy part of town from the blue bloods who lived above.

In sharp contrast, Walnut, Elm, Dietz, and adjoining streets were dominated by mansions and near mansions, some of intricate and elaborate Victorian style, others like brick fortresses complete with towers that resembled medi-eval castles.

These were lived in by the descendants of those who built them with the proceeds from the fortunes they had made locally as hop brokers, feed mill owners, merchants, authors and land speculators.

Other native Oneontans had accumulated great wealth elsewhere. Among them was Collis P. Huntington, who had made his fortune as a railroad robber baron in the west, but much of his vast wealth came back to relatives in Oneonta.

The buildings for what was to become International Business Machines had been located in Endicott, but the founders and the seed money had come from Oneonta and it were already beginning to bear fruit. All told there was a lot of old and some new money in this part of town.

The banks, the better shops, and the churches were on the second level. So were the residences of lawyers, doctors, and politicians. However, they were all subservient to the gentry that controlled the money that controlled the city.

Reaching up the hills that surrounded both the smokey lower deck and aristocratic upper deck, sat rows of modest homes for the middle class who had good jobs that afforded them the necessities of life if not the luxuries.

During the day, Oneonta was three different cultures, but after dark the more adventuresome residents of all three mingled together . . . down where the action occurred, namely below the smoke line.

It is easy to see why Oneonta during the late 20's was once picked by a national magazine as "Sin City" while at the same time it was known as having per capita wealth second to none. Thus its second nickname—"The City of Millionaires."

THE NORMAL SCHOOL

Ever since Otsego County had been settled, women had been the silent partners who bore and raised the children, cleaned the house, washed the clothes, did the canning, cooked the meals, and patched the clothing. Those that married farmers worked in the fields during their spare time.

Parents measured their daughter's success by how high up the economic ladder she married. During a brief period during the 1800's, cotton mills had employed women and children, but as they were abandoned so was any hope for women who wished to work outside of their home.

Steam power began to replace manpower and brain power began to replace muscle power in the mid-1800's, and as the twentieth century approached, it began to influence rural Otsego County. Suddenly, the need for education to meet the new challenge became apparent to local as well as state officials. The rural one room schoolhouse and the "readin 'n 'ritin 'n 'rithmetic" concept was no longer sufficient.

Teachers began to get respect and a living wage. In the past, a seminary (equivalent to present day high school) education was sufficient to become a teacher. Now more was expected of the curriculum and of those who taught it. Intelligent young women who desired to be emancipated and independent flocked to this new growth industry.

To train them, the New York State Legislature had established the Oneonta Normal School shortly before the turn of the century. It was located at the head of Maple Street on the hill overlooking the city, adjacent to what is now occupied by the State University College of Oneonta. It was strictly a teachers training college.

By the time of our story, young ladies from the villages who desired to embark on a career were joined by promising farmers' daughters who wished to escape the drudgery of subsistence farming. Both saw the Normal School as their ladder to success and freedom. There, they could either become a teacher or meet a refined, well educated young man who was one.

Children of college age by the mid-twenties had been born before the war and their formidable years had occurred while puritanical life styles, particularly for females, prevailed. Out in the country they still did. They had been taught that only loose girls painted their faces, that the lips that touched liquor had never touched mother's, and of course that any girl who smoked cigarettes was advertising her availability to men.

Above all, mother had cautioned them that sex was for men to enjoy and women to tolerate, and it should be exercised only as a tool with which to barter in an effort to control their husbands.

It was quite a cultural shock for prim and proper village girls and unsophisticated country girls when they were cut free from their sheltered lives. Now they studied the subjects in the curriculum by day and if they so desired, learned about sex and bathtub gin during the evening.

Some did not give in to temptation, but to many the door to the candy store was wide open and they rushed in. They joined the flappers in the sexual revolution in this sensuous new world.

Young, vibrant, pretty, and out to catch up on what they considered the fun they had been denied in the past, they were the most desired dates by every red blooded stud in town.

Most retained their amateur status but there was tuition, books and clothing to buy; board to pay. A few found it a lot more profitable to have a few drinks and make their charms available to handsome young and wealthy older men than to hoe corn under a hot sun, and more enjoyable to have their own protuberance tweaked than to massage the teats on the dairy cows back on the farm. There were few sources of income for young women and an hour in the sack could net more than a month of "slopping" hogs. What's more, the more adventuresome wanted a well-rounded schooling that included sex education.

GO EAST, YOUNG WOMAN, GO EAST

In tracing Eva's history, it is imperative that any information that came to the press, either directly or indirectly from Eva herself must be questioned. When first apprehended, she refused to talk about her past, but after constantly being badgered by reporters, she relented. It simply was much easier to appease reporters by drawing on her considerable ability as a liar so she gave them all kinds of scoops, none of them even remotely close to the truth.

Her reason was noble. She simply did not want her family name soiled nor her family members humiliated and harassed by reporters. No fox ever covered her tracks to foil the hounds as well as Eva fooled the reporters.

However, the story was just too big. Her mother, Mrs. Margaret Currie, age 68, collapsed and nearly died from the shock when she read in a Toronto newspaper about her daughter's plight. On August 27, 1934, Eva's sister, Mrs. William Baker, wrote for more information and Eva's former husband, Bill Coo (now remarried) wrote to District Attorney Grant. Soon, reporters were getting details from these more reliable sources.

Eva was born in Haliburton, Ontario, a village of 600, 150 miles northeast of Toronto. Her sister, Mrs. Baker, said she was 46 years old at the time of her arrest which would place her birthdate in 1888 although Eva had carved it in stone—her tombstone, no less—as 1885 and, because then as now women seldom overstate their age, we will accept her version. Otherwise, the information that Mrs. Baker and Bill Coo passed on to reporters in 1934 undoubtedly is correct.

Eva was the eldest of six daughters born to Albert and Margaret Currie. They were now scattered all across Canada from Halifax to Vancouver. The union also produced three boys, Bill, Bert, and Ross, still living in Haliburton.

The parents had been strict, religious people, and as Mrs. Baker said, "I can't believe Eva did it; she had a wonderful father and mother and it seems impossible to us that a girl with her background could do such a thing."

Whether it was boredom or rebellion is not clear, but twenty-nine years earlier, at age seventeen, Eva left for Toronto where she trained for and, in fact, became a nurse. It was there where she met Bill Coo, an employee of the Canadian Pacific railroad. After a short courtship, they were married in Spokane, Washington in around 1904. Before settling down in Calgary, Alberta, Eva brought her new husband home to meet her family. That was the last time that they were ever to see her.

Eva said she and Bill were separated in 1918, but others say that the marriage lasted only a few months. All agree that the couple had no children and that Bill was willing to give Eva between thirteen and fourteen thousand dollars in "separation money" in exchange for his freedom.

Already, the two sides of Eva's character were becoming evident. While the Coo's next door neighbor in Calgary recalled her as a "good neighbor" and "kindness itself," Bill recalled that his home mysteriously burned shortly after she walked out of the door.

The family didn't hear from Eva again until "fourteen years ago" (approximately 1920) when she wrote from New York City that she was having an operation for appendicitis and that she would write more later. She never did. Her family made several efforts to find her and advertised for her nationwide to no avail, so they presumed that she had died.

A couple hundred miles north of the city, on the sparsely settled hills in Delaware County, dairy farmers were having a tough time eking out a living. Yet it was not unusual for city slickers to buy the failing farms and operate them profitably. Usually they had a few dairy cows in the pasture in an attempt to fool the gendarme but the cash cow was within the still hidden back in the woods.

Eva, still very much alive, joined this "back to the farm" migration. Later at her trial, Sergeant Murphy testified that she told him that she bought the farm which was located in North Harpersfield between Stamford and Jefferson. Her name does not appear as a "Grantor" or "Grantee" of property in any of the years between 1917 and 1930 in the Delaware County Clerk's records in Delhi. That does not necessarily mean that she did not actually own the property upon which she lived, as many deeds in that period were not recorded. It does mean that we do not know when she took possession.

Newspaper articles that examined her background during her trial are of little help. Reporters, particularly those from distant areas, appear to have gathered their information in bars rather than perusing official records. As an example, one article says that she moved to Oneonta from Stamford, Connecticut. Obviously the reporter heard that she came from the Stamford area and never having heard of Stamford, New York, assumed she came from Stamford, Connecticut.

One newspaper says she lived in Harpersfield from 1924 to 1927. Had the reporter simply checked the Oneonta City Directories, he would have found that her name appears as residing in Oneonta at 29 Chestnut Street in both the 1925 and 1927 editions.

We do know that she was still in Harpersfield in 1924, both from people who remember her there and from the Otsego Clerk's Office where a deed for property on Brewer Avenue (now Woodside Avenue) on the corner of East Street was transferred to Eva Coo "of Harpersfield" from Carl and Lila Van Buren of Oneonta on November 7, 1924. The County Clerk's office shows that she had purchased property in Maryland in 1928.

Most area moonshiners shipped their brew to contacts in the city but Eva was already looking at the more lucrative retail trade. Old Timers remember that while she owned a few cows, she turned the farmhouse, mostly concealed by thick shrubbery, into a roadhouse where she sold alcoholic beverages. While a steady boarder fared well, it was said that railroad men who were just passing through could enjoy a relaxing evening with this pastoral Jezebel as their hostess if they didn't mind waking up in a field, groggy and penniless, the next morning.

This is not the kind of reputation that builds goodwill and repeat business. What's more, she lived much too far from any urban area to attract more than a handful of customers. Oneonta, on the other hand was booming.

The city establishments that sold bootleg liquor and warm feminine bodies had a different set of ethics than those that sold food and clothing. It took a lot of nerve to cut in on their lucrative territory. It also required police and political protection. Eva had the charisma and arrogance, and soon she had the contacts necessary to move into the big time.

To understand Eva's actions during the later period when she was notorious and her every movement documented, it is necessary that we first understand her earlier adventures in Oneonta where she was just one of the many anonymous shadows that prospered in Sin City's underworld, unobserved. For the most part she avoided getting her name in the newspapers during that period. In her business, that was the prudent thing to do.

To fill in the details we must rely on interviews with people who knew her during the period when she was living in Oneonta, plus published accounts written in and after 1934. Many of these articles about her activities show a lack of research and are full of exaggerations. Yet when one dismisses obvious magnifications, a reasonably accurate picture emerges.

Eva lived for the day; she was not an investor. She would not have purchased property on Brewer Avenue for any other purpose than to live there. Whether by design or coincidence, this property was in the respectable part of town, close to the Normal School.

From this vantage point, she and her girls could drive down to Broad Street and cruise the neighborhood doing missionary work among the better class of heathens by pointing out that the same pleasures were available within the discreet neighborhood up on the hill. While there is no evidence that she was among those who employed Normal School girls, she would infer from the house's location that she had the best girls available.

Eva was not there for long and why she left is not known. Her deed contained the standard covenant that said she should "quietly enjoy the premises." It may be assumed that other homeowners in the area did not think that a speakeasy and cat house fell within that provision. Eventually she was to lose her police protection, but it is doubtful that it was this early. What's more, Eva was stubborn, so while unhappy neighbors could have been a factor, it is more likely that she decided that an establishment adjacent to the downtown action would be more profitable.

We hear rumors of other locations (none of which check out) but there seems little or no doubt that Eva worked out of 29 Chestnut Street for the balance of the time she lived in Oneonta. This was within a three story brick building at 25-33 Chestnut Street diagonally across from what was then and still is the I.O.O.F. hall at 36 Chestnut.

On the ground floor was DeAngelos Barber Shop at No. 25; Walsh Bakery at 27; and Opera Pool Room at No. 31-33. Eva's apartment 29 was on the second floor over the Walsh Bakery. There are no known photos of the building which was demolished long ago, but the "newsboy" who delivered the *Binghamton Press* to Eva every afternoon was interviewed and supplied invaluable information about the building, Eva's apartment, and the surrounding community. He also remembers Eva as more attractive than she appears in the newspaper photos. He also found her to be kind. "I remember Eva as a very nice lady; she always gave me five cents for the three-cent paper," he said.

While he was always met outside of Eva's door, he often passed through the pool room enroute to the back alley. The pool hall had the same dimensions as Eva's apartment. These he placed at between 20' and 30' wide and 60' to 70' deep, overall.

To reach her apartment from Chestnut Street, one would walk up very narrow stairs to her kitchen which, along with the adjoining bathroom, took up about a third of the apartment's space. These rooms were at the rear while one or two bedrooms plus a living room overlooked Chestnut Street. A small balcony, where wood, coal, and an ice box were kept, was adjacent to the kitchen and a fire escape led down from there to the alley below.

In every account, Eva is always pictured as operating a "big" full-service house of joy at an upstairs location. The stereotype of a 1925 era brothel brings to mind a parlor, drinks, and hostesses on one floor; bedrooms above. While the word "big" is ambiguous, a 25' x 65' apartment does not fit the bill under any interpretation.

However, on further investigation it is noted that in the 1925 directory, Eva is listed as living at 29 Chestnut Street on the second floor and no one is listed as living in the third floor apartment above. Yet it is unlikely that the apartment was vacant. In the 1927 directory, Eva is still shown as living at 29 Chestnut Street, while Libby Jones lives at 29½ Chestnut Street, which would be the third floor apartment above.

Access to 29½ Chestnut Street was via stairs leading up from the hallway outside of Coo's door. Inasmuch as it is thought that Eva lost protection and scaled back her operations sometime between 1925 and 1927, one can make a case in which Eva operated a traditional two-story brothel in 1925, but had dismissed her girls and simply operated a one-story speakeasy by 1927.

A second and perhaps more plausible explanation comes to mind after we note how Eva operated in her own inn of a size comparable to her Oneonta apartment after she left the city. There, the three girls who were implicated with her in the murder all were independent contractors who solicited sexual encounters within Eva's inn and exercised them in nearby cabins.

It seems reasonable to expect that she had followed a similar procedure in Oneonta and if so, her single apartment was certainly large enough. It probably was not by coincidence that Oneonta's three hotels were each within a stone's throw of her apartment.

The Windsor Hotel at 44-48 Chestnut on the corner of Wall Street was kitty-corner across from her establishment. It was the favorite stopping place for out-of-town drummers when they visited Oneonta. The less desirable, but inexpensive Wilson Hotel at 2 Chestnut Street near Market Street was only a block away, and the Oneonta Hotel was just around the corner on Main Street. Some of her girls also would have had their own apartments nearby. (Two of the three who later were implicated with her in the murder lived at 210 Main.)

Unlike some other area establishments, Eva did not work with street-walkers and she didn't entertain bums. While the Windsor and Wilson would not be apt to turn away any prostitute, even the prestigious Oneonta Hotel would find it difficult to refuse a room to the influential men who arrived with the attractive girls that frequented Eva's place.

Locating in a respectable community on the very edge of the city's ten-derloin shows Eva's business acumen. Details of how she operated her night to night operation are not entirely clear but fortunately neither are they important to our story. The fact that they were so successful that they created a huge cash flow is both clear and important as we soon will discover.

EVA GETS THE BOOT

"Good Time Eva" made a lot of friends in Oneonta. More importantly, she made the right kind of friends—the kind that can shield an unlawful operation.

Her house of joy was a meeting place where an unlikely assortment of people from every walk of life—doctors, college kids, thugs, lawyers, train-men, sweepers and cleaners all rubbed elbows. The businessmen and politicians under whose blessing she prospered, were also there.

Eve knew every colorful personality in the county and colored a few that weren't colored before. She may not have had a little black book, but she had a little black mind and filed there was dirt enough to fill every divorce court in the state.

Given protection, there was a lot of money to be made in her business.

Eva had fallen into a pot of jam and she was eating it up ravenously. The way she purchased cars, furs, and other luxuries is legend.

News about her hot spot traveled rapidly and that was good until it began to reach the city's second and third levels. The wives of married men who enjoyed whoopee and respectability at the same time began to hear about the revelry going on. Attendance dropped dramatically. Eva was becoming a victim of her own success.

Eva's philosophy had always been to live for the day. Fewer patrons were now filling the coffers while mortgage payments, taxes, salaries and other bills were piling up. She saw no recourse other than to call her influential friends, asking for loans.

In Eva's defense, this well may have been an honest effort. After all, she had never turned down a hungry man or anyone who had fallen on hard times. She had always staked any man until his next paycheck was in. However, her new friends were more suspicious. They viewed the calls as blackmail; they began to view Eva as a dangerous woman.

(During an interview, a man who in his youth lived near Eva's opulent establishment and was familiar with it, told us that he "was told" at the time that Eva fell from grace because one of her customers went blind from drinking bad booze in her establishment. Liquor heavily laced with wood alcohol can cause blindness and so, while not confirmed, it is very possible that such an event did happen.)

The bible says, "The Lord giveth and the Lord taketh away." The same can be said about men of influence. Eva was told to shut down her operation and get out of town!!

In the past she had never been in trouble with the law, though many later said that she had insured and killed someone before. However, none of these allegations could be documented or substantiated by known facts.

True, there was the time when a customer refused to pay an upstairs entertainer for services rendered. The girl turned the matter over to Eva who was in charge of accounts receivable. She confronted the freeloader and he answered by throwing her to the floor.

As in a western movie, fists flew, furniture crashed, and the offender fell or was pushed out of the upstairs window. Unlike the stunt men in the movies, he landed head first and his neck was broken. The police had called it an accidental death. No charges were brought against Eva.

Yet at that time she had protection, now she didn't. When she challenged the system by continuing operations, she received an answer in action rather than words. On October 24, 1927 her establishment was raided by Federal Agents and four cases of home brew, fifteen gallons of beer, one gallon of colored distilled spirits and one gallon of white distilled spirits were confiscated.

Subsequently on January 10, 1928, with Don Grant, the same attorney who would later prosecute her for murder, as her counsel, she pleaded guilty in Schenectady to possession of liquor and was fined $425. Eva always kept her money tucked in her stockings. Upon hearing the amount of the fine, she lifted up her skirt a bit, rolled down one of her stockings a little more and took out a roll of bills from which she peeled off the amount of the fine, and stalked out the door.

Outwardly, it was a gesture of defiance. Never within her lifetime had she ever admitted defeat. Yet, inwardly she knew that she would be harassed as long as she worked in Oneonta and she was too smart to let her pride overcome her good sense. Already she was looking for a site outside the city.

On August 14, 1928, she purchased a roadhouse in the town of Maryland from her friend and chief source of liquor, Charles Hamm. Located midway between Colliersville and Schenevus, it was close enough to Oneonta to be readily accessible to the patrons who had not deserted her. She called it Woodbine Inn; everyone else called it Eva's Place.

The inn had a combination kitchen, living room and bedrooms. There was a space for a counter and chairs where patrons could drink their fill, play cards and join in laughter and revelry. A nickel-plated player piano beat out the latest hit tunes.

Freelance "entertainers" moved among the crowd and if a patron became amorous as the evening progressed, Eva would rent, either by the night or the hour, one of her "Blue Moon" cabins that stood to the rear of the inn. In front stood gasoline pumps. Eva still had a following and some of the most influential politicians and socialites of the county still patronized her new place.

Like her earlier establishments, her new saloon catered to people on every step of the economic and social ladder. The elite and the influential received V.I.P. treatment. Farmers and railroad men who flashed large bills might not fare as well. Evidence of this came from a former milk truck driver who related the story of Eva and her Yankee neighbors.

Enroute to his destination in Schenevus, the driver was hailed by Wes Stillman who asked him to ask the troopers in Schenevus to stop by his place, which the driver did.

It turned out that Wes had sold his woodlot for $300 on the previous day and that called for a celebration, so he had spent the night at Woodbine Inn. He was able to successfully navigate home that evening, but when he awoke the following morning, he had a headache but no money.

He reported the incident to the trooper who then continued on to Eva's place. Coo was sympathetic but she had no idea where her patron had lot his money. "He was pretty drunk. I'll bet he fell in the snow and lost it on his way home," she declared. The money was nowhere to be found and it was one person's word against another's. It would appear that all Wes had to show for his woodlot was a hangover, but he was not willing to let matters drop there.

He waited until the next fall when he told several area residents that he had confidential information. When pressed, he gave a date on which he said Federal Revenuers were planning a raid on Coo's inn. The news spread and soon came to Eva's attention. At the witching hour, Wes was sitting up in the woods watching Coo's place. Sure enough, Eva and her entourage were soon busily carrying bottles of moonshine out of the various buildings in her complex and taking them out into an adjoining corn field.

After they left, Wes moved in, gathered up what he considered to be about $300 worth of booze and took it home. Needless to say, he provided the only raid on Eva's place that evening!

Much of her old clout was gone and her enemies reminded her that she was still vulnerable. Woodbine Inn was raided in 1928, after which Eva pleaded guilty to operating a public nuisance and disturbing the peace. She paid a $500 fine. Aside from the two convictions, as far as it is known, Coo had no criminal record.

Of course, occasionally when the young people of the community were having a party, they invited members of the State Police because they would raid Coo's inn and confiscate two or three bottles of booze for "evidence." It was consumed at the party. There were no arrests, no trial, no records. Obviously, Coo never complained; it was just part of doing business in a shady occupation and her contribution to keep her record clean.

Eva's glory days had been in Oneonta but she left while the good times rolled and she brought enough free-spending fans with her to make Woodbine Inn a paying proposition. She would have lived out her years comfortably and died anonymously were it not for an event that, one way or another, changed the lives of every person in every civilized nation on earth—the Great Depression.

When the market crashed on October 29, 1929 it was an omen, not the cause of what was to follow. As it continued to fall, bankruptcies were common and stock prices dropped by well over 80 percent. Industrial output fell to 53.4 percent of capacity and unemployment rose to 24.9 percent. Farm prices dropped from their already depressed levels and while some people went hungry, farmers could not sell some food commodities at any price.

Yet these nationwide figures do not fully assess the damages in Oneonta which had been strictly a railroad town. Of all industries, railroads were hit the hardest. Oneonta's wealthy had owned the blue chips, the growth stocks, the railroad stocks. Many of these securities were now worthless.

Coal was being strip mined and transported by truck. Factories were closed. What few trains that did run carried more hobos than freight. The D&H had many layoffs and did not hire any new men for more than a decade.

There was no unemployment insurance, no Social Security, no welfare as we now know it. People were in shock, confused, despondent. The roof had caved in; the dance had ended and the piper was demanding payment.

It was at about this time that Eva had a personal tragedy. She had fallen in love with Jesse Loucks, a big thirty-seven-year-old man with shiny black hair. He had been employed by the Traver-Mackey Company and more recently by the Texaco Oil Company in Oneonta.

Jesse drank a lot before he met and moved in with Eva. Within the carefree atmosphere of her inn he drank even more. If the *New York Mirror* can be believed, Eva told them that he was a "mean drunk" who had moments of beating her when she was close and throwing dishes and other missiles at her when she was at a distance. That was too much even for Eva, so she kicked him out.

Jesse went to live with his brother at 29 Rose Avenue in Oneonta. On April 9, 1932 he jumped to his death from an upstairs window. Eva, who still professed that she loved him, was devastated.

As if this were not enough, on December 5, 1933, the 21st Amendment to the Constitution was passed. It became legal to sell alcoholic beverages in licensed establishments. Eva, being an old-fashioned girl, continued to sell liquor the old fashioned way . . . without a license. With most bars now legal, the "revenuers" could give special attention to the ones that were not. Patrons who found it socially unacceptable to be caught up in a raid, patronized the licensed pubs.

Eva's place was nearly empty except for the strays she still took in and supported. Five of them were to figure dramatically in her life . . . and cause her death.

FOUR ACES AND A SPADE

The four lost souls, dubbed the district attorney's "Four Aces" by the press, all had been at home in the turbulent waters of the roaring twenties but now were floundering, washed up on the rocks of the Great Depression. The three girls had all been typical "flappers." Now they were unemployed and on public assistance.

Their male counterpart had been a successful salesman by day; a man-about-town, flask toting dandy by night during the good times. Now he was a fading gigolo, a kept man who received room, board and spending money for sharing his paramour's bed.

They were an easy-going, devil-may-care, fun-loving group of derelicts, dominated if not completely controlled by Eva Coo's strong personality and free liquor. Correspondents, at the time, likened them to the characters in Erskin Caldwell's novel, *Tobacco Road*.

However, when the time came when they would be forced to choose between saving their own lives and that of their benefactor, the primitive law of self survival would surface and they would turn on her like the mob that at a later date would desecrate and hang their leader, Benito Mussolini, in a public square.

And what about the Spade? Then as now, he was the forgotten little man in the background; Harry Wright was the victim.

While Eva was the star, these five people played active supporting roles in the grizzly drama. It's important that we understand their history as it was known in 1934.

Martha Clift was born in Honesdale, Pennsylvania on February 18, 1909, the daughter of Edward and Anna (Yeary) Compton.

After she married Harry Clift in Gilbertsville, New York, the couple lived in Butts Corners, New York, but after several moves, they were back in Honesdale where their marriage ended in 1932 although they got back together "as husband and wife" off and on after that.

After her marriage failed, Martha moved to Oneonta. In 1932 she lived with Eva during September, October and November and again in 1933 from June through September. For a while, she lived at 210 Main Street but at the time of her arrest, she was Gladys Shumway's roommate in an apartment at 135 Main Street in Oneonta.

Martha had a daughter, age seven, and a son, age five. She also had an aged, badly crippled mother who lived with her stepfather in an abandoned schoolhouse near Hamilton Farms on the southside of Oneonta. Martha usually left her children in their grandmother's care while she flitted from place to place in and around the city.

Martha wore heavy rimmed glasses and stood as erect as any soldier, which is why she was described as "school teacherish" in appearance. She had dark hair and was of medium height and build. Martha's sensuality, manifested by her soft, low, and gentle voice made her attractive even though she was not physically beautiful. Later, during the trial, she enjoyed the attention she received and was completely composed, never flustered by Byard's tirades.

She had met Eva through her brother, Dick, who was for a time paying attention to Eva. At the time, Martha was a waitress in the Central Hotel in Worcester, New York. Apparently, Little Eva's invitation to join her in a free and easy roadhouse life appealed to her more than standing for twelve hours a day in a small hotel dining room.

Eva's girl friends could make more money in two hours on their backs than in twelve hours on their feet.

Aside from being hailed into court in Susquehanna, Pennsylvania for paying for a car with a forged check, she had no police record. In Oneonta, she had obtained a car from the Dodge dealer with a little cash plus a note that was endorsed with the name Harry Crippen. When Mr. Crippen couldn't remember signing it, the dealer simply repossessed the car and brought no charges against her.

Gladys Shumway had been to the altar twice. Her first husband had committed suicide and she had been separated from her second spouse. She was of average height, with dark hair and a good figure.

Eva claimed that she had befriended Gladys when she was "in a family way." Be that as it may, the two had been acquainted for two years. Gladys lived with Eva from June to September in 1933 and called on her several times a week now that she lived with Martha in Oneonta.

Gladys was the only one of the group who seemed emotional, as evidenced at a later date when she would break down during her testimony. Like all of Eva's friends, Gladys drank a lot and that resulted in her being convicted of disorderly conduct on March 14, 1934. Aside from that she had no police record.

Edna Hanover was a beautiful and vivacious girl any man would love to take to the party but wouldn't dream of taking home to meet mother. In appearance, she would pass as a movie star and at the flick of a photographer's shutter, she would pose like one.

She loved attention and her good looks kept her in the mainstream of the fast life she savored. This flippant, giggling, irreverent young girl, unlike Martha and Gladys, would fit the stereotypical freelance entertainer and hostess one might expect to find in Eva's house of joy.

Edna was born in Afton, New York on November 22, 1911, the daughter of Mr. & Mrs. Howard Butler. She was brought to Oneonta at an early age and attended public schools there.

She had packed a lot of action into a little over twenty-two years. At age fourteen, she reportedly had a child. On November 11, 1927 she married Raymond Hanover, the second of two marriages. It was in that same year that she, along with some high school friends, first visited Eva's establishment when it was in Oneonta.

Attorney Grant (now district attorney Grant) had been her parent's lawyer and therefore represented Edna when her first marriage was annulled. Later, during the Coo trial in 1935, when the defense counsel gleefully brought this to light by asking her, "So you are good friends with District Attorney Grant?," she would reply, "Oh, not too friendly!!" Grant would redden while the farmers and townspeople would laugh loudly.

But, we are now talking about 1934 and at that time, as for the previous eighteen months, Edna had been visiting Eva's establishment, Woodbine Inn near Maryland, three or four times a week except for the twenty-four days she spent in the county jail during March. The offense: disorderly conduct and the use of vile language while under the influence of alcohol. Aside from that she was not known to police officers, at least not officially.

Harry Nabinger was a slender man who appeared to be less than his thirty-nine years. He was quiet, pale and his black hair was carefully groomed back from a broad forehead. Slicked down with the greasy oil so commonly used at the time, it was the first feature one would notice as it shone in any light. His features were regular and when he spoke, his voice was clear and pleasantly modulated.

Within his large, dreamy grey eyes lurked a trace of mystery and misery. Dark, handsome and debonair, Harry was a ladies man. That being his only talent, he used it to become a successful gigolo and hanger on.

He had already failed as a husband and father, having deserted his wife and four children, now ages six through fourteen, in Detroit four years earlier. He also had failed as a Holland Furnace salesman although he occasionally sold Sonophone hearing aids.

As a teenager, he had graduated from the Binghamton, New York high school. He also was an alumni of the Alcoholic Ward of the Binghamton State Hospital, having spent five weeks there in 1932. In fact, if Nabinger had been inclined to tell his story of drunken degregation it would have been unequaled by any of the temperance lectures of Frances Willard's time.

He had known Eva for the last eighteen months, having met her when he was a salesman, and heard that she needed a new furnace for her Woodside Avenue property. He had been living with his sister in Colliersville at that time but having now lost his job, he moved into Eva's bedroom.

There being no law against being a parasite, Harry had no criminal record.

Harry Wright was born October 29, 1880, the only child of Abraham and Hattriet Wright, an old and respected family in the community. They lived in a house that was about three hundred feet behind what is now the village hall in Portlandville, New York.

Harry had big, floppy ears and an aimless grin. As a boy he had few friends and kept pretty much to himself. That might be expected because when he was in the company of his peers he was often the butt of their jokes.

He was adored by his mother but few other people knew that Harry even existed. Apparently, his mother had no camera and everyone else thought it a waste of film to take his picture. At least there are no known photographs of him other than in two group pictures.

In the first, he is among a group of Portlandville Elementary School students. In the second, as a very young man, he stands alone behind scores of hop pickers, almost as though he sneaked into the picture while all other eyes were upon the photographer.

After leaving school, Harry followed in his father's footsteps by becoming a painter and paperhanger. While newspaper accounts credit his intelligence as bordering on retardation, people who remember hiring him during the earlier years, say that he had average intelligence and that he was a real craftsman during the period before he became totally dependent on alcohol.

His father died in 1924 but his mother continued to give him loving care until she passed away in January 1931. By this time, by carefully saving from her earnings as a domestic, she was able to leave her home plus $1,820 in savings accounts to Harry.

This was a tidy inheritance in those days but Hattriet didn't stop there. At the time of her death, Harry, then fifty-one years old, still had not been weaned. Because he was still so dependent on a mother's care, she had made custodial as well as financial arrangements for his future. She had asked her kindly friend and neighbor, Eva Coo, to watch over and take care of him.

Harry already knew Eva and on the day of his mother's funeral, he moved in with her. Having often visited her inn, he probably felt that it was he, not his mother who had died and gone to heaven.

By now, he was stooped, hunched over like a monkey, and he walked with a gait that can best be described as a shuffle. He claimed that his affliction was the result of standing on rounds of ladders during the many years he had been a painter. In truth, falling off of bar stools probably had been a contributing factor for Harry was a drunk, pure and simple.

Coo once remarked, "That baby would drink anything he could lift." Charles Hamm called him "a drunkard who never bathed and who slept in his shoes." People who hired him to paint their buildings said he preferred to be paid in liquor rather than money; it saved the time the transfer would have required.

At the Coo residence, Harry Wright didn't enjoy the privileges extended to Harry Nabinger. He slept on a cot near the back door. He fed the chickens, painted the buildings and did odd jobs around the place. Occasionally, he might paint a building for someone else in the neighborhood, but mostly he drank booze. Yet even Eva's supply was not inexhaustible. She had to lock him out when she left the house in the summer and hide the booze when she left him alone in the winter.

Harry also was good at sniffing it out of its hiding place and when that happened, Eva would pick him up by his ears and cuff him around a bit. The same things happened when he neglected his chores.

Eva's dominant personality would have controlled Wright had he been a sober man; by adding liquor, he was her slave and would do anything she asked without hesitation. One might say he'd give his life for her.

FIGHTING POVERTY EVA'S WAY

Harry's inheritance consisted of $1,500 in a savings account in the First

National Bank in Cooperstown and $320 in a checking account in the Milford National Bank. The duo made regular visits to both banks, always withdrawing, never depositing. The funds in the Milford account were depleted by April 2, 1931 and in the Cooperstown account by October 13, 1931.

Wright had inherited his parents' home and it was insured. The house burned to the ground on June 14, 1933, and Eva came to report the loss on the following day. The pair picked up the $350 check as soon as the claim was adjusted. After considerable haggling, Wilber Portius purchased the lot for $100 ($62.86 by check, $37.14 by paying the back taxes).

By now Harry Wright was penniless so, in December 1933, his benefactor and her boyfriend appealed to Ernie Russ, Maryland supervisor, and Wright was granted public assistance in the form of a monthly voucher for $10 worth of groceries from the S.J. Atwood store in Maryland. The food went to the Coo residence starting on February 1, 1934.

In February of 1934, Mrs. Coo appealed on Wright's behalf, asking that the payment be incrcased. Russ offered an alternative, declaring that it would cost only 27 cents per day to keep him at the County Farm. Coo indignantly refused the offer. After all, she had made a promise to Hattriet Wright to care for Harry and Eva intended to keep her word.

Coo had known and enjoyed the good life. Now she owed mortgage payments and taxes on both her properties and even if she could find a buyer, they would net her less than a thousand dollars. She had not been able to license her car or even buy a battery for it.

Additionally, she was faced with the fact that Wright, previously an asset, had become a liability. Harry, always under foot, was also becoming an irritation. Desperate situations call for desperate measures.

Like a hungry barracuda eyeing a wounded bait fish, she confided in Martha Clift that "Gimpy" would have considerable difficulty in dodging a moving vehicle. Martha agreed.

Having seen no evidence of shock from Martha, Eva put it a bit stronger when, a week later, they were shopping for groceries in the American store in Oneonta. At that point, she said she planned to "bump off" Harry. In subsequent meetings, whenever they were alone, the subject seemed to recur and at each planning session, Martha was becoming more involved until eventually she was an equal participant.

Four plans were considered: (1) To take Harry in a car to the top of a hill, get out and let the car roll down into the river; (2) leave Harry in the car within a closed garage with the motor running while Eva went to the Sidney troopers barracks to provide an alibi; (3) rent the nearby McLaury house for Martha and arrange for Harry to fall to his death while painting it; and (4) run over him until dead and then deposit his body near a busy highway to simulate a hit and run accident.

EVA'S ADVENTURES IN INSURANCELAND

While writing a thesis on the Eva Coo murder, a graduate student at the New York State Historical Association made the tongue-in-cheek statement, "Aside from wanting to insure everyone in sight, Eva was like anyone else." In reality, she did have a few other quirks like rolling drunks and being a madam, not common to the general populace, but it certainly was her fascination with insurance that became her downfall.

It started innocently enough when on October 19, 1931 a $448 policy on Wright's life with Coo as beneficiary was obtained from the Prudential Insurance Company. At that time his date of birth was correctly given as October 29, 1880. That made him fifty-two years old at the time.

When Coo became a student of insurance she found that it would be to her advantage if he shed five years. On some policies, double indemnity would not be paid to those over fifty; on others, less than double to those over fifty; and on still others a medical examination was necessary for persons over fifty; and on all policies, the premiums were less on men under fifty years of age.

Therefore, before going on an insurance buying binge, she decided to take some mileage off of Harry's life. Martha Clift was asked to and did bring the Wright family bible up to date by writing in the names, date of birth and date of death of some of the Wright family whose names had not been recorded. Next, she added "Harry Wright - born October 29, 1885" as the final entry.

Town clerks did not record birth records in 1880 so there was no way that there would be a contradiction there. However, in the Portlandville cemetery there loomed a large contradiction cut in granite.

On May 20, Eva and Harry Nabinger stopped to see Arthur Stanley, a seventy-six-year-old Scottish carver and sculptor who lived in Worcester. She told him that she wanted "Eva Coo - 1893" added to the Wright family stone and while he was there he might as well correct Harry Wright's birthdate to read 1885 instead of 1880. They agreed on a price of eight dollars and, on June 2, 1933, Mr. Stanley changed the cipher to a five on Harry's birth and added Eva's name and birth, as instructed.

On June 1, 1934, armed with the family bible as evidence, Coo convinced the insurance agent that a mistake had been made in Harry's age on the Prudential policy and the birth date on the policy was changed to 1885 as soon as the paper work was completed. The amount of coverage was increased to $602.

Coo and Nabinger combed the papers, looking for the names of insurance agents that they might contact. Coo always insisted that Nabinger write the letters because she said that his penmanship was better than hers. Nabinger signed them "Harry Wright." At the trial he insisted that this was at Wright's request and Wright was not there to deny it.

While everyone else in the county was trying to avoid insurance agents, Eva was welcoming them with open arms and free drinks. Yet some agents were more frightened by Eva's reputation than by not meeting their quota. Gladys Shumway told Albert Bell, her insurance agent, that a friend who lived at "the first Colonial gas station on the left side of the highway past Cooperstown Junction" wanted insurance and that the place would be "brilliantly lighted." She didn't mention Eva by name. When Bell went to call, he recognized it as Woodbine Inn and hit the accelerator instead of the brakes. Some others just didn't get around to following up on the lead.

On advice of one insurance agent, Coo visited Edward R. Campbell, a Schenevus attorney, on May 21, 1934. He concurred in the opinion that the surest and best way to make the conveyance from a policy was to show the estate as the beneficiary and then a will to distribute the estate's proceeds. After hearing that Wright's only living relatives were two cousins, he wrote the will with Coo as sole beneficiary and Wright signed it. After that, all new policies gave Harry's estate as beneficiary.

During July of 1933 an additional two policies of $190 each were placed with Prudential and shortly after that, three with Metropolitan Insurance Company. Between March and May of 1934, Coo took out almost a dozen policies on Wright's life, bringing the total to twenty. By now she didn't think he was worth much alive, but she knew he was worth $12,900 if he died as the result of an accident.

Coo not only plastered Wright with policies, but also had them on five other people—Harry Nabinger, Gladys Shumway, Martha Clift and Martha's two children. Most of them, too, carried double indemnity.

The only person not insured would appear to be Eva herself. However, as the plot unfolds, one will note that Eva had the best policy of all . . . one might call it her "Umbrella Policy" because, while she masterminded every detail, she managed to get other people to implement those plans. She believed that if something should go wrong, that would be her insurance against being held accountable.

On June 6, 1934, Eva and Martha sentenced Harry Wright to death. Even after having been born again, his new fiftieth birthday was drawing near and after it passed, his value would depreciate by nearly fifty percent. Because they were not sure that the first three plans would qualify as accidental death, they decided to implement plan number four by simulating death on a heavily traveled highway via a hit and run driver.

CRUMHORN MOUNTAIN

Otsego County nestles in the foothills of the Catskills where paved roads run up fertile river valleys with mountain ranges towering up on each side. A maze of narrow dirt roads, like spider webs, dissect the hills that separate each valley.

Eva's new establishment was located on the paved highway between Binghamton and Albany, about eight miles northeast of Oneonta. As though it were an omen of the part it would play in Eva's future, the Crumhorn cast a dark shadow over her roadhouse, shortening each day.

Both the townships of Maryland and Milford dissect the Crumhorn, an area that was the last land in the area to be settled. It is called "Crumhorn Tract" on the earliest maps of the county, so while history does not record the origin of the name, the story that Sir William Johnson, under royal patent, granted it to a man named Crumhorn from Columbia County, seems to be most credible.

It is said that Sir William characterized it as "a worthless piece of land created by the Almighty for wild beasts and rattlesnakes." Either Sir William was a poor salesman or he made his famous utterance after he unloaded it. No one got rich and famous by living there but perhaps its harsh environment made those born there appreciate the opportunities that they found elsewhere.

The first settlers had moved into Otsego County before the Revolution but with the Indians siding with the British, the migration ended. After the Cherry Valley Massacre, the few settlers who remained made a hasty retreat back to civilized New England. It was not until 1785 that a few hardy souls ventured back into the area.

However, once the migration got under full swing in the early 1800's the population grew rapidly until, by the period immediately following the Civil War, it reached a peak that would not be surpassed during the next one hundred years.

Many early settlers favored the hills. Some came to escape malaria and that disease was spread by anopheles mosquitos that frequented the swamps in the lowlands. The valleys were forested by white pine that was slow to decay whereas the hills were mostly covered with hemlock which was easier to clear. Game was more plentiful along the valley streams so the Mohawk and Iroquois did most of their hunting there, seldom frequenting the hills. Perhaps most of all, there was a lot more vertical than horizontal land so it was much less expensive.

During the early years, work was done by hand with the aid of oxen and horses. They could function on a rugged hillside as well as on the level valley terrain. By the 1920's, however, farms were becoming mechanized. Mowing machines and reapers had replaced scythes. Corn was cut by harvesters and blown into silos instead of being cut with a sickle and shocked in the field. Tractors were beginning to replace horses. The price of farm produce was so low that it was no longer possible to make even a subsistence living without the use of machines which were not compatible with rocky hillsides. On the other hand, work had been plentiful and wages high in the cities; hillside farms were being abandoned at a rapid pace.

The Depression was the final death knell. By 1934, land that never should have been cleared in the first place was reverting back to brush, and buildings were falling into decay. Some dirt roads were being abandoned; the rest seldom traveled. This was true of the rural areas in much of upstate New York but it was particularly true on the Crumhorn. The very features that make it a desirable place with a spectacular view for the homes that now dot the area, made it a tough place to make a living in 1934.

Now forgotten are scores of Horatio Algers who in earlier days left the Crumhorn and found their fortunes elsewhere. The Crumhorn is now best known for Eva Coo who went there to make her fortune—and failed.

DOOM STALKS THE REHEARSAL

On the afternoon of Decoration Day, May 30, 1934, Eva suggested to

Harry Nabinger that it was too beautiful a day to sit inside. "Let's take a ride," she suggested. Harry agreed. Gladys Shumway and Martha Clift were at the inn and they were invited to join the party.

When Eva said she would like to visit the place where Clara Meyers once lived on Crumhorn Mountain, Harry was a bit apprehensive. He had been on the Crumhorn only once, but once was enough for him to realize that the roads were steep and narrow and he wasn't sure that his balky old Dodge was up to it. He finally gave in.

Eva knew exactly where she wanted to go and it wasn't where she had indicated. Instead, they took the shortest route to the abandoned Scott farm. All the road names have changed since the 1930's, but driving it today one would proceed onto Buriello Road (which was practically unused at that time). It was the loneliest of all lonely places on the Crumhorn.

The only person living even remotely close was Harry Zindle. His home was about a half mile away on a deadend spur off of Buriello Road. Harry worked on the WPA project that was improving the Portlandville School lawn part of the time, was on public assistance part of the time, and was a wry-faced, dry-humored rustic all of the time.

While the Wightmans, who lived over two miles away, owned and worked the land across from the Scott farm, the Scott place itself was abandoned and growing up to brush. Several outbuildings were in varying stages of decay, but the spooky old farmhouse had not totally given up to the elements. The lawn and driveway were covered with knee high weeds. Small wonder that it had the reputation of being haunted.

The property was owned by Mrs. Iva Fink, daughter of Nellie E. Scott. She now lived in Milford, some seven miles away. Iva had lived there with her parents until 1912 at which time she had married Ben Fink, a former carpenter. Her parents left it in 1930 and no one had lived there since.

As Nabinger's car reached the Scott house, Eva suggested that they stop, so Harry drove into the driveway. The four of them got out of the vehicle and walked around the premises. Eventually, they went into the house.

Eva blew dust from the keys of a decrepit organ before sitting down to play a few lively selections. Even though the result was wheezy at best, it brought some relief to the somber surroundings.

Various discarded implements were examined but only an old heavy oak mallet was removed from the table. Eva left it outside on the porch. "Wouldn't that be something to hit someone over the head with?" Eva remarked to Gladys Shumway.

The sun was now dropping below the horizon and the cool night air began to bring a welcome respite to a humid day. The three women sat down on the steps and each lit a cigarette while Nabinger went to the car, draped his torso over the steering wheel and waited for their return.

Bats emerged from the upstairs windows and gracefully began their nightly mission of sweeping the area free of insects. The setting reminded the girls of tales they had heard about the "haunted house" and they took turns in relating them and laughing at their absurdity.

Suddenly, Gladys stopped in mid-sentence and silently pointed. An object . . . in the failing light it was hard to tell whether of human form or an apparition . . . was quietly passing by. The women arose, walked to the car and the group drove back to the inn, perhaps a bit apprehensive, but certainly not realizing the significance of what they had observed.

Eva Coo
Oneonta Daily Star

Harry Wright at age 18.
Courtesy of A. Bullard

View in 1934 of Coo's route (now Peterson Road) up Crumhorn Mountain.

Scott house with "X" indicating where Wright died.

The death car in the Scott house driveway.

Interior of Scott house (note mallet on cabinet).

Woodbine Inn

Trooper K.B. Knapp points to spot where body was found.

Martha Clift and Eva Coo at their arraignment.

Albany Times Union
Martha Clift

Albany Times Union
Harry Nabinger

Albany Times Union
Eva Coo in her cell in Cooperstown jail.

PART TWO

LADY LUCK

Fred Palmer was a farmhand employed by Eva's next door neighbor, Clara Meyers. His father died and Fred, accompanied by Harry Nabinger and Eva Coo, attended the funeral in Binghamton on June 6. However, Eva's mind was on a funeral she was planning rather than the one she was attending. Consequently, on the return trip, she stopped at Morris Peak's garage in Franklin to inspect his cars. She stated that a friend was in need of a good used vehicle.

Peak had a 4,000-pound Willys Knight on the lot and he was asking $200 for it. Eva was impressed and told the dealer that she would send her friend over to give it a trial run. She had already determined that she did not want to implicate her boyfriend by using his car and, in addition to being short of cash, another reason why she had not used her own license was so that it could not be tied to her victim's death. Franklin seemed far enough away for the car to be unidentified and two tons heavy enough to carry out its purpose.

During the next few days, Martha and Eva laid the final plans. Clift would drive the car with Coo and Wright as passengers. They would enter the Scott farm driveway, continue into a field and turn around, then come back into the driveway opposite the house. At this point, Martha and Harry would exit while Eva got behind the wheel. Martha would walk with Harry in front of the car, and when he was correctly positioned for the kill, she would signal by lighting his cigarette. (The pair must have had a feeling for the melodrama where the condemned man always had his last cigarette before the firing squad snuffed out his life).

Financial arrangements were also discussed. Eva had told Clift that there was less than two thousand dollars in insurance and there was some overhead (namely a funeral and burial) involved. The two agreed that Martha should receive $200 for her part, and with it she would buy the death car from Peak.

Coo, as chief executive officer of the enterprise, had loftier tastes. On June 13 she, accompanied by Clift, visited Pontiac Sales in Oneonta. Harry Clement gave the girls a demonstration in a new Pontiac. They drove to

43

Worcester and back. Coo showed satisfaction with the car's performance and indicated that she might purchase it in the near future.

First, however, she would like to see how it performed on Franklin Mountain and she drove it, alone, to Franklin. There, she stopped at Peak's garage and told the proprietor that on the following day, a lady would pick up the Willys Knight and drive it to Oneonta so that her mother could inspect it. On her return trip she left fifty cents with Martha Clift for bus fare to Franklin in the morning.

On June 14, Martha picked up the car a little before noon and she took Gladys Shumway for a joy ride in Oneonta. After dropping Gladys off, Martha drove on to Eva's place, arriving there at about 1:30 p.m.

The two women proceeded to Worcester where Eva purchased some groceries while Martha met Levi Gallup and had a few drinks with him in a local tavern. Levi left, Coo returned, and the ladies had another drink or two before they started home to pick up Wright. Upon arriving, they parked the car behind the inn out of sight of the Meyers home which was only 500 feet away.

Harry was busy painting the porch when they drove up. Eva said that she wanted some of "the prettiest little cherry trees that you've ever seen" and that they were free for the stealing up on deserted old Crumhorn Mountain. Harry, like a puppy dog, followed her to the car and climbed into the back seat. Eva tossed in a blanket, and as planned, Martha drove.

Harry was told that inasmuch as they were taking some trees without permission, they should keep out of sight. Whenever they passed a building, pedestrian or car, Eva ducked down so that she could not be seen and she instructed Harry to do the same. Martha later testified, "By this time Harry got pretty well learnt and got down on his own hooks without being told by Eva."

As the Scott farmhouse came into view, so did the first disappointment because "Cy" Wightman, with the aid of a team of horses, was working in the Wightman field across from the house. Unobserved, the troop sat in the car out of sight and smoked cigarettes while making small talk.

As chore time approached Cy left, and when sufficient time had elapsed for him to be out of sight, Martha started the car and drove into the driveway. That's when Eva, without warning, switched the agreed upon plan for one of her own. She hopped out of the moving car, ran to the house and returned. At the trial the prosecution would contend that she now had the mallet under her sweater, and as she approached the car, she beckoned to Harry who disembarked and joined her in front of the vehicle, which was slowly moving in low gear. Supposedly, the mallet descended, there was a push toward the wheel tracks, and poor Harry's chest was crushed under the weight of a two-ton vehicle.

Martha, in nervous excitement, continued to drive out into the lot and returned as originally planned. At the trial, Deputy Sheriff Owen P. Brady testified that Eva told him that even after this massive mutilation, weak and wasted old Harry was able to mutter, "My God, I see why you got me here now."

By pure coincidence, it was on the same afternoon of June 14 that Ben Hunt decided to drive up on the Crumhorn to look at the Miller farm which he had heard was for rent. His wife Clara and the Hunt's five children came along to enjoy a pleasant afternoon ride. They asked Iva Fink, the owner of the Scott property, to join them and she brought along her little boy.

As Eva and Martha drove along Buriello Road near Harry Zindle's house, they saw him and two of his five children walking along the road, and so they stopped to chat. Mrs. Fink previously had asked Harry to keep an eye on her property so Harry was quick to point out that he happened to walk by the old house at dusk on Decoration Day and had observed a car parked in the driveway. He suggested that they get over there to see if anything had been stolen by the intruders. Hunt cut the conversation short and headed for the haunted house.

By now, darkness had enveloped the deep valley and was creeping up the hillside. At the very moment that the Willys Knight sedan reached and straddled the body, the headlights on Ben Hunt's car broke over the top of the hill. Hunt quickly drove down to block the driveway. Eva, afraid that the body was not completely covered by the car and tall weeds in the driveway, shouted to Martha, "Back up six inches." Authorities estimated that had the Hunt car arrived just one minute earlier, the occupants would either have seen the murder or prevented it!!

Mrs. Fink, soon joined by Mrs. Hunt, rushed up to the death car, demanding to know why the women were there. Eva quickly explained that she had stopped to relieve her bladder and pointed out that Martha had not even stepped out of the car. Mrs. Fink didn't buy that explanation.

There were sharp words between the two parties because the house owner thought that the trespassers were there to steal. Mrs. Fink knew Eva but not Martha. At one point, Eva said that she had enough without stealing from anyone to which Mrs. Fink replied, "I should think that you would have enough of everything considering the business you are in."

Mrs. Coo gave the women a flashlight and asked them to look inside the car which they did. They saw a quilt, two bags, and a man's hat. They went to the house and found it was locked. Hunt, still suspicious, sarcastically observed, "You did a good job" in the belief that somehow, the intruders had been in and out without breaking the lock.

Only when Coo and Clift were briefly separated, did the latter show a bit of weakness by saying that she was from Bainbridge and had only recently met Eva and didn't want any trouble. Eva in seeing a solo conversation, rushed over to bring it to a sudden halt by pointedly reminding Martha that "I didn't do anything you didn't do!!"

At this point, both Coo and Clift coolly suggested that the property owners call the state police if they did not believe their story. Was this a diabolically clever maneuver, the height of stupidity or the zenith of bravado?

After all, there was nothing that Coo and Clift wanted to see more than the Hunts and Finks driving away regardless of their mission. Yet, with a car full of adversaries, would they have left without one or two of the adults standing guard over their prisoners until the police arrived? More likely, it was a bluff. How often does a criminal want the police called to the scene?

Ben Hunt had remained in the car caring for the children, but he took down the license plate number from the Willys Knight. He was impatient because it was getting close to the time for the Baer-Carnera fight to be broadcast. He backed the car up enough to let the trespassers depart, but Coo and Clift simply sat in their vehicle, showing no indication that they planned to leave.

Finally, to break the stalemate, Martha walked over to the other car and said, "She's stubborn, you know, and you made her mad calling her a thief; please go on and I'll get her right out of here." This was enough to satisfy Ben who quickly headed for home.

Just as quickly, the Willys Knight was driven forward enough to reveal Harry's body which was quickly wrapped in the blanket and dragged onto the back seat of the car. Martha, again at the wheel, headed for Eva's place, taking the most direct route.

"I wonder if he's dead," Coo inquired as she turned around, placing both knees on the seat and peeking under the blanket. "Harry!" she called out. There was no answer.

If Clift's later testimony can be trusted, she suggested that they take Harry to the hospital, but Coo refused. When they were 939 feet west of the inn, they stopped and Eva dragged the corpse out of the car and into the ditch ten feet from the north side of the highway while Martha watched for oncoming cars.

The duo then continued on to the intersection of Routes 7 and 28 in Colliersville where they turned the car around at Shepherd's Gas Station. Once home, Eva handed Martha one dollar for gas and instructed her, "For God's sake throw out that quilt."

In Oneonta, the blanket was tossed over the fence at the intersection of Grand and Prospect Streets. Upon arriving at their apartment, Clift confided to Gladys Shumway that "Eva Coo has killed Harry Wright" and she made Gladys promise to say that she had been with her all day.

Martha, accompanied by Gladys, then drove the car back to Franklin, arriving there at a little before 10:00 p.m. As soon as the Baer-Carnera fight was concluded, Mr. Peak brought the pair back to Oneonta where they stayed with Gladys' mother overnight.

A WOMAN'S WORK IS NEVER DONE

Eva Coo had completed a full day's work by any standard when she entered her inn that evening, but it was only the beginning.

She had a good relationship with her sixty-five-year-old neighbor, Clara Meyers and Clara's hired man, Fred Palmer. Eva bought her milk from Clara and often borrowed her Model T Ford; Clara often used Eva's telephone.

In her absence during the afternoon, Fred had attempted to return one of Eva's cake tins and Clara had come to use the phone. Both found the place locked.

At about nine o'clock, seeing that the lights were now on, both came over to complete their missions; of course Eva had to explain her absence. While she said that she had gone down to "Pop's Place" to buy cigarettes, should anyone else inquire to please tell them that she had been home all afternoon. Both promised, not realizing that this would be more than a little white lie. After placing her phone call, Clara went home, but Fred stayed on.

Eva told her visitors that Harry Wright had left at seven p.m. to visit James Johnson in reference to painting one of his buildings and would be returning with Harry Nabinger. On several occasions she walked to the window and looked down the road.

At about 9:30, Edna Hanover arrived and she offered to look for Harry. Eva knew that when the authorities emptied his pockets, they would find his watch which had stopped at 10:22. She certainly didn't want anyone finding a dead body while it was supposed to still be alive so she suggested that Edna might better help her with the ironing while they listened to the Baer-Carnera fight.

At 10:30, Eva showed greater concern, even though she said that Harry had probably tarried at Johnson's home or stopped in with Nabinger at Pop's Inn for a few frosted ones. She asked Fred and Edna to drive down and check out both places.

When Edna's Ford coupe returned and its occupants said they could find no trace of Wright, Eva went to the phone and called Trooper W.B. Cadwell in Schenevus, telling him the same story and asking if there had been any reports of accidents that night. Cadwell jumped into a troop car, blowing the horn as he passed the inn, so that Eva would know that he was looking for Harry. Shortly afterward, he returned and announced, "I have found him."

Eva asked, "Where?" to which the trooper replied, "Down the road struck by a car."

"Is he hurt bad?" Eva's voice was trembling.

The policeman replied, "He's stone dead."

Eva exclaimed, "Oh, my God!" and slumped down in a chair.

At this point, Cadwell phoned Trooper Ernest Knapp and joined him as well as Dr. E.C. Winsor, acting coroner, at the site where the body lay. The coroner's verdict was accidental death via a hit and run car, and as the watch found on his body had stopped at 10:22, that was given as his time of death.

Cadwell returned to talk with Coo in reference to the disposal of the body. Eva said that she was the beneficiary of a "small" insurance policy that should cover the cost of burial. Edna Hanover tried to interject that there was more than "a little" insurance. She was later to testify that Eva was talking so fast that she was unable to convey that information. After the trooper left, Coo cautioned her not to mention that to anyone.

Coo directed that the body be picked up and taken to the R.V. Tillapaugh funeral parlor in Schenevus. This was done.

As if the night was not hectic enough, Mickey Gaffney and a friend stopped to rent the Blue Moon cabins for the balance of the night. It was understandable that she turned away the business.

This conversation was hardly completed before Eva received a phone call from Harry Nabinger. She gave him the news and it was quite evident from the conversation that he was too drunk to drive so she told him to wait and she, Fred and Edna would come to Oneonta to bring him home.

Earlier in the day, Nabinger had borrowed Clara Meyer's Model T to go to Andes on business. After running a few errands in Oneonta, business was forgotten and he spent the rest of the day and evening bar hopping. Now, near midnight, he had called to say that the car he had borrowed had stalled. The trio found it parked in the middle of Main Street across from the post office and Palmer pushed it to the curb.

While the trio was looking for Nabinger, he pulled up in Jim's Taxi, which he had employed to "push the car home." Eva and Fred eventually were able to get the key from a very intoxicated Harry, and Fred finally got the car started and drove it home.

Nabinger rode back with Eva and Edna. In her later testimony, Hanover said that Harry kept arguing with Eva who was trying to tell him about Wright's death. At one point, he said "You think you're so smart; I saw him five minutes before he was killed and he wasn't killed where he was found."

Eva, visibly stunned replied, "My God, Harry, do you know what you are saying?" Harry's statement, made in a drunken stupor was to cause him a lot of grief at a later date while undergoing hours of cross examination by Coo's attorney.

A fear of death also lurked in his muddled brain. According to Edna's further testimony, while Eva was trying to get him in the car she said, "Walking and staggering all over the road like that, you'll get hit with a car."

Nabinger replied, "If I get hit with a car, you won't have to hire anyone to kill me." That utterance also was to haunt him because Byard was to later use it in an effort to show that Nabinger (also insured by Eva) must have known that Wright was marked to die via an automobile because now he was worrying about an accidental death.

No one will ever know how well Eva slept that night. However, the events of the day would justify sweet dreams. Perhaps she dreamed of sitting in the midst of an economic desert, but on the horizon saw an oasis with a sign welcoming her to "fat city." The highway was straight and her new fire engine-red Pontiac had a tank full of gas that would speed her down the highway back to "the good life" she had once known.

True, the day had started off on a horrendous note, but "all is well that ends well." The victim, a derelict, with no close relatives, often staggered up Route 7 and the odds were that he would eventually come up second best in a joust with a passing car. Apparently the acting coroner and the troopers, all acquaintances of the victim, thought so as they prepared their reports.

Ignored were a few facts. There were no skid marks, no broken glass, a crushed rib cage with ribs penetrating the lungs and heart indicated that the body had been run over, not struck down, and there was no blood on the road or in the ditch. Harry's watch had stopped at 10:22, just before Eva had sent the state police looking for him, yet rigor mortis had set in when he was found minutes later. And what about the watch? The time was noted, but not noticed was the fact that it had stopped by being wound too tight some time earlier, not from the sudden jolt of an accident!!

The expected had clouded all eyes against seeing the obvious. With the police and coroner both reporting an accidental death, Harry was about to be planted and Eva was about to reap the harvest.

HASTE MAKES WASTE . . . . AND INDICTMENTS

On the morning of the 15th, Eva had a few odds and ends to attend to. First, she called on Meyers and Palmer and again cautioned them that there might be some questions asked about "the affair" and her whereabouts the previous day. If questioned they were to say she was home all day, came over for milk at six p.m. and that Meyers accompanied her back to the Coo residence to make a phone call, and that Palmer stayed there until 3:45 the next morning. She also invited them to the funeral.

Next, she borrowed the Meyers car to make the funeral arrangements. She told Tillapaugh, as she had the troopers, that Harry had "a small" insurance policy that would cover his funeral expenses and she took along a policy for four hundred and sixty dollars to show him that he would be paid.

She asked that the casket be the same as the one in which his mother had been buried, but when she learned that it would cost two hundred and ten dollars, she decided on a cheaper one stating that it seemed foolish to bury so much money. Tillapaugh was not used to dickering with the bereaved and suddenly found himself accepting an offer of one hundred and fifty dollars for the cheaper model and a lower stipend for the minister's praying over poor Harry's corpse. Wright had no suit, so Coo left one of Nabinger's for his burial.

That afternoon, Eva called Martha and when she entered the inn, Eva said, "Did you know that Harry got killed last night?"

Martha replied, "Did he? That's too bad."

Martha appeared calm and was playing the game well. After she left, Eva started calling the insurance agents, telling each of them about Wright's untimely death. Everything was going smoothly.

Unknown to Eva, dark clouds were forming. Ben Fink, who had been away on a drilling job on the fourteenth, heard his wife's story and he filed a report with the state police. This report of simple trespassing, by itself would have been relegated to the circular file. However, as soon as Eva became a suspect, this statement identified the murder weapon and placed the perpetrators at the murder scene and would, therefore, become Eva's death warrant.

However, on the 15th, Eva was not yet a suspect and the trespassing report and the hit-and-run report might not have been connected were it not for someother incidents.

So who did break the case? Authorities disagree but most historians give credit to Earl Ames, the Metropolitan Life Insurance agent who responded to Eva's call on the sixteenth. While seeking her signature as beneficiary, he noted that she was very nervous, her hands shook and she perspired freely.

He journeyed on to the funeral parlor and conferred with Tillapaugh who also was skeptical that the cause of death could have been as stated on the coroner's report. Before leaving the funeral home, Ames made a phone call to the coroner in which he said, "Dr. Getman, I know that you have given a verdict of accidental death in the case of Harry Wright, but I would advise you to reopen the case. There are some things that don't look right to me."

The funeral was held as scheduled and, afterward, Dr. James Greenough performed an autopsy and determined that Wright could not have died as the result of a hit and run accident. The error in determining the cause of death was not Dr. Greenough's only discovery. In fact, the first thing he noticed was that Harry Wright was wearing one of his suits!! In fact, the label inside the jacket still bore his name!! This certainly demands an explanation. Wright did not own a suit, and as previously noted, was buried in one that belonged to Nabinger. According to one of the persons we interviewed, Mrs. Greenough told her that the suit in question had been donated to Christ Episcopal Church in Cooperstown and placed in their rummage sale. Nabinger, usually unemployed, must have obtained it there. Coo in turn, left it with the undertaker to clothe Wright.

A reporter from the *Oneonta Daily Star*, "Gunny" Gunther, now picked up the story from Ames. Originally, the death had not even been worth a single paragraph on the back page, but now it made the front page headlines. Most "old timers" who are interviewed give him the gold detectives star, and indeed a detective magazine at the time gave him credit and a monetary award for his accomplishments. A radio and TV show, "The Big Story," sponsored by Pall Mall cigarettes, gave him nationwide prominence for his "scoop."

The newspaper headlines alerted Sheriff George Mitchell who said, "It looks fishy to me" and began his own investigation. He was joined by state and city officials. The *Star* gave Mitchell credit and he was interviewed by several detective magazinesand praised for breaking the case.

Today, given the advantage of historical perspective, it would appear that Eva herself should receive credit for breaking the case; it was her greed in applying for insurance benefits before Wright's body was hardly cold, and while damaging evidence was still warm and just begging to be noted, that really did her in.

For Coo, Sunday June 17 was the last "day of rest" on this earth. At a party at Pop's Inn that evening she, along with Nabinger, Hanover and Jim Johnson reviewed past events. Coo had received the personal effects from Wright's body, namely one watch that had mysteriously been wound too tight to function. It was given to Johnson. Coo also conferred with an undertaker seated at another table, asking him some general questions about autopsies and whether traces of alcohol and poison could be detected after embalming.

On Monday the 18th, the victim was buried in the Portlandville Cemetery. Eva, Harry Nabinger, R.V. Tillapaugh and Mr. Sexton, the cemetery caretaker, were the only ones in attendance.

At five p.m., Coo was taken into custody, ostensibly to give information for the coroner's inquest in Cooperstown. Clift was taken to the police station in Oneonta. Both were questioned for the next thirty-six hours without being charged with any crime. Coo knew most of the officers and the district attorney who had in fact represented her on three previous occasions. However, she was badly outnumbered. As one trooper reminded her, "Don't think that you can tire us out—there are ninety-five of us."

By now, the connection between the report of trespassing and homicide had become apparent and Troopers Cadwell and Knapp were at the Scott farmhouse. However, they did not see a connection between the murder and the mallet and did not fingerprint it.

Nabinger, Shumway, and Hanover were questioned. Unable to raise $5,000 bail each, they were held as material witnesses in the Otsego County Jail.

On Tuesday the 19th, while Eva and Martha were being interrogated in jail, Troopers Ernest Maynard and Kenneth Knapp went to the Coo residence on orders of District Attorney Donald Grant. Without her knowledge and without a search warrant, they removed the screen and raised a sash, thereby breaking into Eva's bedroom. There they found the deed to Wright's cemetery lot and three or four insurance policies.

Their work was interrupted when Sgt. John (Jack) Cunningham arrived to say that Owen P. Brady and Joe Mitchell were on the way with Eva so that she could feed her parrot, dog and cats. The troopers hid in the nearby McLaury barn until she had left.

Going back to the dresser drawer, they found that the policies had disappeared. Upon further examination they were discovered under a pile of clothes within a locked closet leading off from the bedroom.

In the darkness of their new hiding place they had even reproduced. Now there were fifteen policies. Some were on the lives of Clift, Clift's children, Nabinger, Shumway and Coo herself, but most were on Wright. They seized the policies as evidence.

During later illegal searches, additional policies were found and from time to time during the trial and always over Byard's objection, introduced into evidence. A total of twenty of these policies were on Wright's life.

While waiting for the district attorney to arrive, Trooper Maynard busied himself by feeding raisins and bread to Polly the parrot. Polly, who had a vocabulary that included every four letter word known to mankind, was a big attraction at the inn and second only to Nabinger in Coo's affections. Maynard's action not only desecrated Eva's sanctuary, but killed her cherished pet. During our interview, one lady remembered that visitors had always been greeted by Polly who was perched next to the door. "Come in, come in, come in," she would squawk, usually accompanying the invitation by flapping her wings in a motion simulating a gesture toward the inn's inner sanctum.

During the trial, Coo's attorney argued that the illegally obtained evidence should not be considered, but Judge Heath in his charge to the jury explained, "Now something has been said about illegally obtained evidence —for instance insurance policies. Our courts have said and I deem it my duty to charge you it is the law, that evidence obtained for instance without a search warrant may be legal evidence and properly received as evidence in a trial if it be otherwise competent. The court has permitted the receipt into evidence of insurance policies alleged to have been found in defendant's possession at her roadstand—they may be considered by you as legal evidence."

THE NEW MEN IN EVA'S LIFE

Before going any further, you should know a little more about several men within whose hands Eva's fate was to rest.

Donald Grant, an ambitious forty-two-year-old district attorney was about to try his first case of first degree murder. However, he had previously vigorously and effectively prosecuted and received convictions on two second degree murder charges—Edna Coolbaugh of Cooperstown, who fed her baby arsenic so that she could spend more time with her lover, and James Webb of Gilbertsville who had killed his mother with an axe as she lay sleeping in bed.

Dark, sleek, square of chin and usually dressed in somber blue, this ambitious young Republican would not let anything stand in his way of a conviction and if that was to help him climb the political ladder, so be it. Hard working, meticulous, calculating, even ruthless, he knew exactly how to fit together the wealth of evidence available to him. This was his one opportunity to show his considerable talent to a national audience and he had no intention of letting it pass him by.

James J. Byard, Jr. was born in Oaksville on January 15, 1872. Following his admission to the bar in 1900, he practiced law in Cooperstown for twenty-three years. In 1923, he moved his offices to Oneonta.

While Everett C. Holmes was first appointed to defend Coo, he was soon joined by Byard, and from that day on it was "Sunny Jim's" show.

His father, James Byard, Sr., had been a realtor; his mother was the daughter of Judge Gorham, so perhaps his talents in the field of law had filtered down through the family genes.

A lifetime Democrat, he ran for Surrogate in 1906 and in 1912, he was defeated when running for Congress by only 700 votes. Coming this close in such a solidly Republican county was quite an accomplishment.

A big, bearish man, reporters compared him with Lionel Barrymore in appearance. He was a lawyer of the old school, blustery, clever and a real spell-binder. His reputation went far beyond Otsego County, in fact he was considered one of the shrewdest lawyers in the state. Although he had made many court appearances and successfully represented many clients in criminal cases, this was his first murder trial.

Only one clergyman ever visited Coo in her Cooperstown cell. Reverend

Harry Brooks, a former Milford Methodist minister, drove up from his charge in Susquehanna, Pennsylvania. He didn't stay long and he didn't return. After all, why would she need help from the Almighty when she already had Jim Byard in her corner? Eva Coo knew that she had the best mouthpiece in the country and she trusted him as completely as Wright had trusted her.

Yet at a later date, Eva was to condemn Byard as a traitor. Many say that no lawyer could possibly have defended her more skillfully, yet a few imply that he was just another tie in the railroad. Let's delay our opinion until all the evidence is in.

Riley H. Heath presided over both the Grand Jury and the session of the Supreme Court in which Eva was tried. Heath, a six-foot, middle-aged, bronze-faced Ithaca resident was noted for being a strict disciplinarian in the courtroom.

In any trial, the judge can have a great deal of influence on the outcome as he controls the conduct of the attorneys and determines what evidence can and can not be considered under the law. He also charges the jury, telling them how to view the evidence in light of the law. Ordinarily he has a great deal of latitude in determining the punishment after a conviction although, in this particular case, death by electrocution was mandatory for conviction of first degree murder.

His career is far less affected by the outcome than is that of the attorneys although his skill will determine to a great extent whether or not an appeal will be granted.

(George Tillapaugh, son of the funeral director, when interviewed, remembered an incident when he entered the courtroom after all the seats were occupied. He climbed to, then sat on a narrow window sill. During part of the proceedings, he lost his balance and fell into the aisle creating considerable commotion and a stern rebuke from the judge.)

George Mitchell was born in Morris, New York in 1886. He and his parents moved to Cooperstown two years later in order to join the family's livery business which consisted primarily of moving freight from the railroad and trolley lines to various stores. As trucks replaced horses, they added taxis, school buses and household services.

Aside from a healthy interest in police work, George had no practical experience in the field. That was the norm, not the exception for most people who sought that office in those days.

In 1932, he ran for sheriff, the top law enforcement office in the county. The sheriff's duties also included caring for the prisoners in the county jail and overseeing the welfare of jurors when court was in session.

Mitchell was well-known, well-liked and respected. For a Democrat to be elected as sheriff was unheard of in Otsego County. Democratic governors have appointed Democratic sheriffs to fill unexpired terms, but George Mitchell was the only Democrat ever to have been elected by the people in Otsego County.

Detractors may say that he rode in on the coattails of Roosevelt's landslide, but there have been other Democratic presidential landslides and they didn't bring in a Democratic sheriff. Obviously, the voters felt that George Mitchell was competent to do the job. He took office on January 1, 1933.

GHOULS TAKE OVER THE CRUMHORN

After thirty-six hours with little or no sleep, Clift confessed at the Oneonta Police Station at 3:30 a.m. on Wednesday, June 20. Upon hearing the news in Cooperstown, Coo said, "She's squawked, I'll tell the truth" and her statement was taken at 8:30 a.m. The confessions were nearly identical except that Clift claimed that Coo drove the death car; Coo, that Clift was the driver. Coo also made no reference to the mallet.

The district attorney believed Clift and offered her absolute immunity in return for her statement and co-operation at the trial. It was this carrot as well as fatigue that brought Martha to her knees.

Eva, on the other hand, had spent too much time studying insurance and not enough time studying law. Because she had fooled Martha into driving the car, she was sure she could not be held, at least not for first degree murder. She told Don Grant, "You can't convict me of murder, Martha drove the car." This misconception of the law plus the fact that people of influence wanted to roast Coo, not Clift, were lessons she was to learn the hard way.

During the trial, Coo's attorney was unable to prove that the confession was obtained under duress and it was allowed in evidence. Later in his charge to the jury, Heath said, "Eva Coo is indicted as a principal to the causing of Wright's death by the use of an automobile. What is a principal? Our statute says—I am quoting now—'a person concerned in the commission of a crime, whether he directly commits the act contributing the offense, or aids or abets in its commission, and whether present or absent, and a person who directly or indirectly counsels, commands, induces or procures another to commit a crime is a principal.' "

With the confessions safely in his pocket, Don Grant petitioned Justice Riley H. Heath to convene a special Grant Jury. Heath signed the order on the same day he received it.

On Thursday the 21st, Everett C. Holmes, a former Oneonta City Judge, was assigned as counsel for Coo and Clermont G. Tennant, a Cooperstown attorney, for Clift. However, neither was informed of the ordeal that was in store for his client late that afternoon.

At about 7:00 p.m. each prisoner was loaded into a separate car, Coo's driven by Owen Brady. Neither was told where she was being taken, but as they passed Portlandville, Coo commented, "I know where we are going and I'm glad for I was going to ask the district attorney to let me go up there and show him just what happened." They arrived at the Scott farm at 7:45 p.m. to simulate the time that Wright had been murdered.

Dr. Winsor, District Attorney Grant, Undersheriff Brady, Coroner Getman, Sheriff Mitchell, Dr. Greenough and R.V. Tillapaugh, mortician, were in attendance. Early that morning, upon order of the district attorney, but without any court order, the body of Harry Wright had been dug from his grave and taken to Tillapaugh's funeral home. At about noon, it was transferred to Crumhorn Mountain and parked in the woodshed behind the haunted house where it remained until about 7:00 p.m.

As though from the script of a bad movie, with darkness closing in, a storm headed up the valley. Claps of thunder roared and bolts of lightning pierced the sky. As the rain began to fall, a ten minute recess was taken within the Scott farmhouse. Once the rain stopped, the re-enactment resumed.

In the driveway was the death car, and behind it, Harry Wright's coffin. It had been turned over and his partially decomposed body lay on the upturned bottom panel. Grant asked Eva to shake his hand, according to most sources, although at the trial, this was disputed. Grant then asked her to put the body in the car. This, she said she did, "the best I could." Sheriff Mitchell suggested that after handling the body, she should wipe off her hands on the grass.

The body was moved from place to place in the driveway and the clearance of the Willys Knight noted. Only the car lights and bolts of lightning illuminated the grizzly scene.

Grant asked Coo to drive the car. At one point, it slid to the side and the

D.A. said, "You almost did that the other night," to which Coo replied, "I wasn't driving the other night."

Both Coo and Clift withstood this ghastly ordeal for four hours. During the trial, the State called this event a re-enactment of the crime; Byard more accurately referred to it as "one of the most ghoulish third degrees in the history of any land" and asked, unsuccessfully of course, for the district attorney's arrest.

The following day, Troopers Knapp and Cadwell took the mallet (which Eva had been asked to identify at the re-enactment) to the district attorney to be held as evidence. At the trial, Byard unsuccessfully contended that this evidence (the mallet) was a plant. Was he right?

Up until now there was overwhelming evidence that Eva planned every detail of the murder, but absolutely none in which she was physically involved. Under the law she could be convicted without physically participating, but could she be convicted of first degree murder in the eyes of the jury? Could that be why, suddenly, the prosecution found evidence that would change Eva from a passive planner to an ax-wielding demon?

During the initial investigation there were probably two mallets within the Scott farmhouse, but no one considered any mallet as evidence. No fingerprints were ever taken from any mallet. During the trial, two troopers as well as the Finks and Hunts identified and placed in evidence a mallet and Clift claimed that it was wielded by Coo during the murder. Yet, Harry Cross, an Oneonta policeman admitted as a defense witness, that he had taken the original mallet home as a souvenir. This 3½-pound oak mallet was considerably heavier than the one that was at the trial identified as the missile that Eva wielded. The matter of mallets was, is, and always will be controversial. Many historians doubt that any mallet was on the porch the night of the murder nor that Eva could have obtained one from inside the locked building in the short time allowed. This is further discussed later in our story.

The re-enactment had not reinforced Clift's statement so, as soon as the party returned to the jail in Cooperstown, Grant again questioned her as to who drove the car. Finally, at 4:15 a.m. on the following morning, Saturday June 23, Clift admitted that she had been the driver. At this point, Grant demanded that Clift surrender the original agreement and he charged her with first degree murder, but signed a waiver in which he promised to allow her to plead guilty to second degree murder which would carry a twenty-year to life sentence if, during the trial, she would "tell the truth."

On this same Saturday, a coroner's inquest was held at which time Sheriff

George Mitchell's deposition was heard and Coo signed another confession. However, during the trial Judge Heath did not allow this second confession to be submitted as evidence on the grounds that he could not determine whether it had been made at the coroner's inquest held on that date, and he was giving her the benefit of the doubt.

BYARD COLLIDES WITH A STONE WALL

Cooperstown is the "Birthplace of Baseball" so it probably was appropriate that there was a judicial double-header on Monday, June 25. At 8:30 a.m. Coo and Clift were arraigned before Justice of the Peace Harold D. Carpenter. Before that was over, the Grand Jury convened in the courthouse at 10:30 a.m. One newspaper billed the dual happening as smacking of "Jersey Justice."

At the arraignment, Sheriff Mitchell entered his deposition, supported by affidavits from Coo, Hanover, Nabinger, Mr. & Mrs. Fink, Mr. & Mrs. Hunt, Winsor, Cadwell, and Clift. Coo, represented by Holmes, and Clift, by herself, both entered pleas of not guilty and were escorted to the Otsego County Jail.

At the courthouse, the selection of Grand Jurors was under way; twenty-two were sworn in and from them sixteen would need to be present to form a quorum, and twelve vote in the affirmative in order to indict. The entire body was sworn in by County Clerk Hintermister.

Bail of $5,000 each was set for Nabinger, Hanover and Shumway and as that was far beyond their reach, they joined Clift and Coo, both held without bail, in the county jail. Even though the Grand Jury had not yet deliberated, District Attorney Grant, confidently predicted that the trial would start on August 6th.

As she entered her cell, smiling brightly, Coo joked with her guard, but looked a little distressed when she heard a newsboy shouting, "Murder! Extra!" on the street outside. She asked jailer Murphy to bring a paper to her cell. Clift, on the other hand, entered her cell showing no emotion whatsoever.

During the next three days Grant brought thirty witnesses before the Grand Jury, and on June 29 the jury brought in separate indictments charging each woman with first degree murder. Coo and Clift, through their attorneys, again pleaded not guilty and continued to be held in the bastille. Heath thanked members of the Grand Jury and sent them home but did not discharge them, in order to save the taxpayers money, should the group need to be recalled.

Byard immediately asked that Coo and Clift be tried together. Grant said they had been indicted separately and should be tried separately. He had good cause as Clift was his star witness.

Byard asked for a change of venue to Tompkins County, quite rightfully arguing that Coo was a notorious character who could not possibly get a fair trial on her home turf. (This was a clever maneuver because Judge Heath's home was in Ithaca, Tompkins County.) Grant disagreed.

Byard asked the D.A. for an admission that he had offered Clift immunity in exchange for her testimony. Grant refused. Byard countered that if it were not forthcoming, he would ask to review the Grand Jury's minutes. Grant again refused.

The judge indicated that he saw no merit in any of Byard's proposals, but that he would give a final verdict on August 6. In the meantime, he asked that Byard serve these and any other motions on Grant ten days before that time.

There was, however, complete agreement among all the attorneys on one point—that the county pay them for their services. Clift had no funds while Coo had property worth about $1,000, but it would net only about two hundred dollars after mortgages were paid. She had no liquid assets. Heath determined that the county would pay one thousand dollars each plus expenses to Clermont G. Tennant to represent Clift, and James Byard, Jr. and Everett B. Holmes to represent Coo. Heath set August 6 as the date that the Supreme Court would convene in Cooperstown and August 13 as the date that they should begin taking evidence.

On July 2, Holmes and Byard filed a demurrer to the June 29 indictment. Besides claiming several technical errors, they complained that one person (Coo) could not be charged with a crime for which another (Clift) had been indicted; also that Judge Heath had not even been in Cooperstown at the time the Grand Jury considered the case and so the court was not in session, thus the indictment illegal.

On July 6, while a defiant Eva Coo sat in her cell within the grey stone prison walls, her Woodside Avenue property was transferred to Mrs. Niver, Holmes' secretary, and her Maryland property to Charles Hamm.

It was on this same date that Byard added to his complaint the fact that the Court of Appeals in the case of the People vs. Van Wormer, had formed a precedent, namely that "it was there held that no one can be compelled to be a witness against himself (Constitution Article 1, Section 6)," and furthermore that, "the compulsory oral examination (doubtless written also) of persons before trial or upon trial for the purpose of exacting unwilling confessions or declarations implicating crimes can not be used."

Byard and Holmes were not getting any sympathy from the court and it was no better within the jail. For a brief period they had been given permission to interview their client in private. However, they complained that on and after July 25, one of the sheriff's underlings always stayed five or six feet away from the defendant, and from that vantage point could hear every word that was spoken.

In his deposition, Holmes said in part that when "He requested that the attache, hireling or sleuth from the sheriff's office, leave the room as he (had) some important conversation to have with the defendant relative to her defense, said attache or sleuth refused to do so, insisting that he was under direction from the sheriff not to permit anybody to talk to Eva Coo in private, not even her attorney." The affidavit asked that the attorneys be allowed to confer with her in private.

Justice Andrew McNaught of Stamford acted upon the request as follows:

"Ordered, directed and decreed that Everett B. Holmes, or his associate counsel James J. Byard Jr., may at any and all times between the hours of 9 a.m. and 6 p.m., interview and have consultations with Eva Coo at any place in the jail or courthouse as to them may seem the most fitting place for a consultation and interview with their client, and that the sheriff, his attaches, hirelings or sleuths be and hereby are forbidden to be in the hearing of the defendant or her attorney, and it is further

"Ordered that said interview may be had in the courthouse in the village of Cooperstown and said interviews are to be private, not to be eavesdropped upon by any attache or sleuth of the sheriff's office or district attorney's office, and that said attorney may interview her at length at such times as they may deem necessary for the preparation of her defense in the above entitled action; however, the defendant is not to be let out of the custody of the sheriff, and that he is to see that she is not permitted to escape from him, but nevertheless, the defendant's attorneys are to be entitled to interview and converse with the defendant without any interference or eavesdropping whatsoever and the sheriff of the county of Otsego is hereby directed to bring the defendant Eva Coo to some convenient place where she can be interviewed in privacy by her attorneys, and without any interference whatsoever by physical appearance or eavesdropping by the sheriff or any member of his force or any sleuth connected with the case."

A layman could have said all this with, "Permission granted," but presumably the defense savored every word of this lengthy decree because it was about the only favorable decision they were ever to hear and even this one came from a judge not connected with the case.

As promised, Superior Court convened at 10 a.m. on August 6. Coo, all "dolled up," was there to watch the proceedings. The defense formally made its motions. The judge denied a change of venue, overruled the demurer, and modified McNaught's order. Byard submitted a motion to inspect the Grand Jury's minutes and it was allowed with the consent of the district attorney. A panel of two hundred prospective jurymen was drawn. The defense made a motion, asking that an order be granted allowing them to exhume Wright's already desecrated body one more time, the purpose to allow expert physicians to discover if there were any head wounds.

On the seventh, another one hundred prospective jurors were called and an order allowing Wright's body to again be brought to light was issued.

On August 11, Jesse Spargo and Albert Young dug up the body. In attendance were Dr. Harry L. Cruttenden of Cooperstown and Dr. George W. Augustine of Oneonta, representing the D.A., and Dr. Norman W. Getman, coroner, Dr. E.C. Winsor, Schenevus and Dr. James Greenough for the defense. At 10 a.m. the coffin was opened and quickly closed. The mutilation of two previous autopsies plus the passage of time had brought about an advanced state of decay. There was unanimous agreement that an examination would be futile.

Already, it was time for witnesses to appear at the trial and Byard still had little to work with. He had dislodged only two boulders from a stonewall —and one of them had fallen on his toe.

COOPERSTOWN BECOMES COOSTOWN

For countless ages mankind has been fascinated by, rooted for, and made folk heroes of misfits they "wouldn't be caught dead with" at a social gathering. Examples can be cited going back to the dark ages, but in the interest of brevity, let's leaf through the pages of time to the days of our own "wild west."

Even then, to become a folk hero one needed a good public relations agent as well as a nasty disposition. The James brothers, Billy the Kid and other assorted assassins would have died with no more recognition and no more sympathy than their victims, were it not for the several writers of dime novels and song writers who glamorized their brutal deeds.

By the 1930's, this task had been taken over by the detective magazines and newspapers (particularly the big city tabloids). They had a huge and receptive audience. The country was in the throes of the depression, but even the unemployed had five cents with which to buy a newspaper and plenty of time to read it.

Through the media, the daily exploits of such gangsters as "Scarface" Al Capone, "Legs" Diamond and "Dutch" Schultz were followed, much as sporting events are today. Outlaws like John Dillinger, "Machine Gun" Kelley, Bonnie and Clyde, and Ma Barker and her boys all had a following. Even common murderers (preferably of the female gender) like Ruth Snyder made big news.

Otsego County was then, as now, a safe and sane county in which to live. Even so, there had been some relapses over the past 140 years and scores of people had paid for their gory misdeeds with their own lives. In fact, one Otsego County man, George Brazee, had been put to death in the electric chair on December 15, 1921 for the murder of his former wife near Elk Creek, only eight miles from the Scott farm "haunted house."

Yet, never before had any Otsego County murder received more than passing local attention. No one knows why news people from distant points were first drawn to the Eva Coo trial like flies that feast on carrion, but as soon as the Associated Press and Universal News picked up on it, all the major newspapers nationwide followed by sending their best reporters.

It is doubtful that even the most clairvoyant journalist could have realized that he or she was there to report on a homicide so bizarre that it would make criminal history, but whether by insight or good fortune they had picked a winner.

No product can be successful without the proper packaging, and as soon as the opportunity arrived, Eva became a product to be marketed. A graphic example is her "before and after" photographs. The ones taken by the police at the time of her arrest show a tough, defiant, unkempt middle-aged outlaw. Photographs taken after her attorneys were assigned show an attractive, respectable, motherly looking matron.

The tabloids and detective magazines saw in her a witch . . . a woman of mystery . . . an attractive woman who controlled men . . . a vamp . . . a woman betrayed . . . or whatever else their editors thought would sell on the corner newsstand. While the local country newspapers stayed close to the facts documented in court records, the more sensational city papers sometimes valued a melodramatic story more than an account that can now be used as fact.

Long before the trial began, reporters were arriving. One landed on Otsego Lake by seaplane, thus himself becoming a story in the local papers.

Reporters must send back stories to their editors even when there are none, and during the period when both the defense and the prosecution were preparing their cases in private, there was nothing new to report, so they were called upon to get "human interest stories."

Dorothy Kilgallen, one of the "sob sisters" who covered the case, spent a night in the "haunted house" to get some atmosphere.

One press photographer visited Harry's grave in Portlandville. A small girl was playing among the monuments in the local cemetery. The enterprising photographer recognized the opportunity to add drama to an otherwise dull scene. Grabbing the bouquet of flowers that adorned a nearby tomb and with it in one hand and a dime in the other, he persuaded the girl to kneel down prayerfully, as she gently and reverently placed the flowers on Wright's grave. The picture was a classic and it was widely distributed. Even now, poor Harry could get no recognition unless it was artificially staged and news people were doing some ad-libbing when the script was dull.

Traditionally, murder suspects hide their faces. During the Coo trial, it was the local visitors. Whenever Eva was paraded past a group of local onlookers, either within or outside of the courthouse, she would slowly walk by, calling each man by his first name as though she was walking up the receiving line after a wedding. Few managed to avoid recognition and more than one husband had some explaining to do at home after one of these exhibitions.

People were covering the courthouse lawn, trying to catch a glimpse of Eva as she took her morning walks within the confines of the prison courtyard. Reporters could do much better than that; they could interview the notorious one in person. Many of them did, making Eva a legend in her own time . . . or maybe it was in her own eyes. All this attention seems to have blinded her to reality before the trial was under way.

As previously mentioned, after the interviews some reported that she was a sinister, calculating "roadhouse vamp"; one called her a "Hillbilly Diamond Lil" who "once dominated a household of dependents and n'er-do-wells." One said she was a good-hearted woman now "repudiated by the lover whom she supported, by the scarlet woman she sheltered during the birth of an illegitimate child, and by her closest friend, Mrs. Clift, who turned states evidence to save herself." Some saw her as defiant; others as good natured. They all saw a confident woman, willing to talk abut the case although not about her family.

She seemed to enjoy the attention she was receiving and the stories that resulted from her interviews, although at one time she said, "One dare not even think in the presence of these reporters."

Yet, when news people were present her tongue was sealing her death warrant. During one interview she was quoted as saying, "I may discuss the private lives of some of our famous citizens. I know about things they do when their wives aren't around."

Although this may have been in jest, with Byard already under pressure from the "famous citizens," it was not making his work easier nor her life expectancy greater.

It was at about this time that he scolded her for talking to news people. She replied, "Aw, now Jim, don't scold me. They talked to me. You're bawling me out, eh, Jim?" Byard, unable to retain a pompous attitude, laughed.

However, it's doubtful that he saw much humor in the fact that Eva was becoming intoxicated by the celebrity status she was enjoying from the press. This attention, more stimulating than wine, was smothering her inhibitions and loosening her tongue.

Sober men of influence who worked behind closed doors with no reporters present, became even more concerned than before. The evidence was overwhelming, but "the wheels of justice grind slowly."

Eva's day in the sun would be short lived.

THE JURY

In the courtroom, grey-bearded judges of a bygone age sternly looked down from heavily framed pictures as they had on lesser proceedings for many years. Below, sat the current judge, bailiff, and other court officials, as well as a few family members of prospective jurors and curious spectators. Attorneys for both the state and the defense were there to make decisions that would be the difference between life and death for Eva, who sat with her attorneys. From her cell, separated from the courthouse by a courtyard, Martha could look out of her window and catch fleeting glimpses of the melodrama in which she would later become a crucial part.

The judge asked to hear from those jurors who wished to be excused from duty and after hearing various reasons, forty-five of the first one hundred men were allowed to leave. For the first time in the history of murder trials, at least within the state of New York, instead of examining each of the remaining talisman individually, the jury box was filled with twelve men at a time and they were questioned collectively as far as was possible. The press was told that this unusual procedure was employed in order to save time. As the story unfolds, it will become evident that it was certainly not the only device used to rush Eva through the formalities on her journey to purgatory.

It is interesting to note that although a woman could die for her crime, no woman could sit in judgement. By law, only men who were under the age of seventy and were U.S. citizens and Otsego County residents could serve on a jury. Of these, only taxpayers were considered.

Reporters for city newspapers were shocked to see the informal rapport between the attorneys and the laymen. One commented, "Lawyers called the prospective jurors by their first names, asked about their crops, their families and their stock. Jurors often called the attorneys by their first names and chatted with them during the examination." Country newsmen understood rural ways and that any attorney who gave the impression that he felt superior to his country cousins would have a difficult time in pleading his case.

One prospective juror was quickly dismissed after he volunteered the information, "I believe she's guilty. I used to visit her place."

In order to weed out others who were less willing to talk, Eva took an active part in the selection, often whispering advice, sometimes vigorously objecting to prospects. Her attorney listened. After all, she had spent a lifetime sizing up men and had a wide knowledge of the habits and opinions of the county's male population.

By 3:15 p.m. on August 15, the last of twelve jurymen plus two alternates had been selected. They were:

Alonzo Hood, 66 years old, laborer/farmer, West Burlington
Jesse Newkirk, 61 years old, laborer, Oneonta
Henry Konofske, 62 years old, laborer/farmer, Fly Creek
Robert Jones, 49 years old, farmer, Edmeston
Harold Hill, 30 years old, farmer, South New Berlin
Ansel Aylesworth, 38 years old, farmer, Edmeston
James Ainsle, 46 years old, farmer, Hartwick
Robert Morton, 60 years old, farmer, Middlefield
Robert Halbert, 38 years old, farmer, New Berlin

Harvey Meacham, 64 years old, farmer, Burlington Flats
Felix Rode, 31 years old, farmer, Fly Creek
Byron Waffle, 49 years old, farmer, East Springfield

Alternates
E.J. Monroe, 60 years old, farmer, Schuyler Lake
Clyde Pittsley, 27 years old, trucker, New Berlin

While the area was predominantly farmland, a large segment of the population lived in Oneonta and Cooperstown. Residents of these population centers, as well as the towns of Maryland and Milford, were challenged in the selection of jurors. Aside from one farmer who lived outside of the city of Oneonta, all jurors came from the most rural parts of the county, quite distant from Eva's operations, so an all-farmer jury with conservative views resulted.

Heath welcomed the jury by saying, "Do not think we are locking you up. Enjoy yourselves. Laugh and chat; get plenty of exercise. You are good sports and good citizens and I appreciate what you are doing."

During the period of the trial, they were housed on the top floor of the Fenimore Hotel. Being farmers, they were active people who didn't sleep late due to the lifelong habit of rising early to milk the cows. One of the first things they did was to organize a quartet, and their favorite song, "Red Wing," often wakened other guests as the sun's early morning rays first welcomed the dawn.

When not on active duty, various sheriff's deputies including Harry Freeman, Bernard Carr, and Earl Gallup tried to keep them from getting bored by taking them on trips and to various entertainments.

On several occasions they attended baseball games during the day and saw movies at Smalley's Theater at night. They took field trips, including an inspection of the O-te-sa-ga Hotel and the Ambrose Clark Iroquois Farm Estate to inspect the sheep and cattle. They attended a band concert, and when there was nothing else to do, were taken on nightly automobile rides. Under supervision, those who wished to do so were allowed to attend Sunday church services and to be visited by their families. During Heath's illness, each was allowed to spend a half day at home.

During the trial they were alert, attentive, and conscientious as they evaluated the evidence.

Otsego County Courthouse

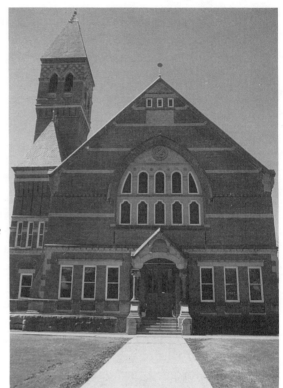

Oneonta Daily Star

Undersheriff Brady, Sheriff George Mitchell, Deputy Sheriffs Hannahs and Joseph Mitchell.

Eva Coo and Mrs. George H. Mitchell, jail matron, as they enter the courthouse in Cooperstown.

Oneonta Daily Star

Oneonta Daily Star

Two of several poses Eva struck during the trial proceedings.

A posed courtroom scene with L-R: Joseph Deery, Don Grant, Jim Byard, Jr., Nick Sterling and Eva Coo.

Judge Riley H. Heath

Donald Grant, D.A.

Dr. Norman Getman, Coroner

NYSHA Library Special Collection

The jury.

Oneonta Daily Star

The jurors were taken to a baseball game for relaxation.

A re-enactment of the crime on Crumhorn Mountain, June 21, 1934.

Spectators were admitted to the courtroom through a ticket plan.

Defense witness, Harry Zindle, sold these souvenir mallets.

Journal American *reporter, Dorothy Kilgallen, spends a night in the "haunted" Scott house.*

Harry Ransom Humanities Research Center
Univerisiy of Texas at Austin

*Seaplane which brought reporters
to the trial in Cooperstown.*

Courtesy of Will Richards

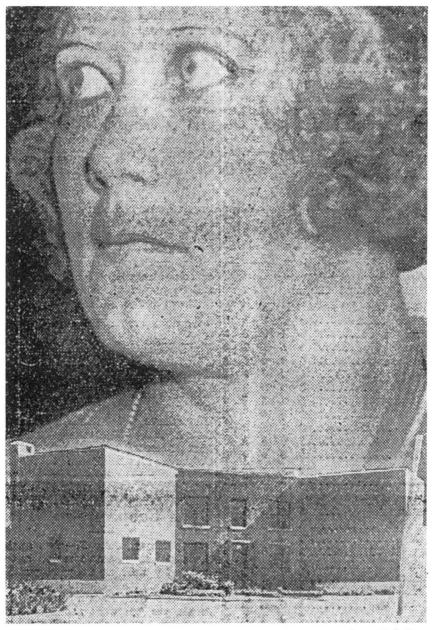

Oneonta Daily Star

Eva Coo and Sing Sing Prison.

PART THREE

"LET THE GAMES BEGIN"

Coo was now receiving fan mail from all over the United States and Canada. A lot was of a spiritual nature and included religious tracts that explained how to save her soul if not her body. Because her image had been painted in brighter colors in more distant climes than at her home base, most letters expressed sympathy for her plight, with only enough hate mail to add spice. All incoming mail was censored; there is no indication that she answered it, but if she did, that mail too would have been censored.

On August 13, the first day that the Supreme Court was in session, there were only seventy-five onlookers and the majority of them were court officials and news people. During the next few days, there were only twenty-five spectators in court.

On the 15th, the jury started hearing evidence and there were more spectators including such notables as Frank J. Loesch, chairman of the Chicago Crime Commission and member of the Wickersham Commission on Crime.

Loesch followed the trial closely and at the conclusion was quoted as saying, "My experience and what I have read leads me to believe that this is probably the first case in criminal history in which two women unaided by any man have committed murder for a pecuniary gain."

By the 16th, only persons over the age of eighteen were allowed to enter the upstairs chambers which were crowded to capacity with about as many men as women in the audience. After the seats had been filled and the comfortable standing room had been occupied, no others were allowed to go into the courtroom where the trial was being conducted.

These people milled about on the first floor and on the courthouse lawn, waiting to replace any who left the proceedings. For most, this was an idle hope because many spectators kept their seats during the noon recess, having brought box lunches with them. They ate while chatting over the morning's proceedings.

By the 17th, the crowds increased, people now arriving at 7 a.m. and filling the room by 9 a.m. The *Oneonta Daily Star* reported, "It is decidedly not a Cooperstown audience, there being, as one accustomed to the local faces looks over the room, only here and there a face that is familiar. Another paper said that of the 600 people in attendance, only fifty were locals.

At noon, the courtroom was cleared and those people who had brought their lunches in order to be on hand for the afternoon session, were compelled to seek a pleasant spot on the courthouse lawn. During the midday recess, Sheriff Mitchell had the building swept and fumigated. After the safe seating and standing capacity of the chamber had been taken up for the afternoon session, the outside doors were once again closed to the public.

By the 20th, hundreds of cars, the majority from out-of-state and out-of-county, were roaming the streets seeking parking spaces, and a thousand visitors were lined up at the entrance to the courthouse by 6 a.m.

Those that were turned away, flocked to the courthouse lawn. There was a gala atmosphere with vendors selling balloons, ice cream and souvenirs. Perhaps the most ingenious was Harry Zindle, the man who by being in the right place at the right time had set the wheels of the "Black Maria" rolling over Eva's future in the first place.

When not testifying during the trial inside, he was hawking his home-made souvenir mallets to the crowd outside the building, with a spiel that went something like this: "Only a quarter folks. Made of wood from the haunted house on Crumhorn Mountain. Buy a mallet like the one Eva Coo used in the murder of Gimpy Wright." It is reported that he sold 500 outside the courthouse plus others in gas stations in nearby towns.

Crowds continued to increase and come earlier each day. In order to give as many as possible a chance to see the proceedings, Sheriff Mitchell issued tickets. Those waiting unsuccessfully to enter the morning session of the court were given tickets for the afternoon session. Those who attended morning sessions were given tickets for the following morning if they wished but had to take their chance on gaining entrance after those disappointed in the morning had been seated. Tickets for three days were produced to accommodate those unable to return on successive days, and upon request, one entitled to a morning ticket was given a choice of three days, the same procedure being followed for afternoon tickets.

Meanwhile, for several weeks there was a steady stream of traffic heading up the winding roads of Crumhorn Mountain. When their cars reached the crossroads in front of the Wightman home, most of the curiosity seekers came to the door to seek directions to the haunted house. After Daniel Wightman tired of being an unpaid traffic cop and tour guide, he constructed a road sign in the form of a mallet, painted it fire-engine-red and pointed the handle (in the form of an arrow) up the road that would take the sightseekers to the Scott farm.

The *New York News* of August 26 reported even more festive activities. They said, "At the notorious gas station on the Albany-Binghamton road where Harry Wright had tended chickens and did painting for Diamond Lil, a hilarious party was staged by passing automobilists. One woman played the piano, while arrivals sang 'That Old Gang of Mine'."

Meanwhile, Jim Byard reported that every day he was in receipt of a half dozen or more letters from all localities inquiring as to the possibility of purchasing Eva's Woodbine Inn property.

There were even more lookers than prospective buyers. The *Oneonta Daily Star* reported on August 31 that, "Hardly a day passes without a sizable number of visitors there, the parked cars along the road, at some times suggested that a serious accident had occurred. It is estimated that there were nearly 100 of the curious there at one time last Sunday."

The *News'* flair for the spectacular would indicate they broke in and took over the premise, but Charles Hamm, formerly one of Coo's suppliers, now owned Woodbine Inn and it seems more likely that he welcomed and profited from the gala event.

The item went on to say, "Atop old Crumhorn Mountain, even more exciting scenes were enacted. Mrs. Iva Fink, present owner of the Old Scott homestead where Wright was supposedly bludgeoned and run down, auctioned off family heirlooms. Old walnut picture frames, almanacs and paperback novels perused by former habitants of the deserted house were sold for sums far in excess of their value as antiques.

Back in Cooperstown, Eva sat in court, her former smile visibly faded as the evidence against her continued to mount. At first blush, it would appear that her peers were dancing on her grave. Yet, were Eva free to attend her own wake, it seems likely that she would have been the one to organize the party. She surely would have been the one to sing the loudest and pass out free drinks for everyone.

FRIENDS DESERT A SINKING COO

During the trial, reporters saw what they perceived as rats, squealing in order to save their own mangy hides as the mother ship foundered against the reef of hard evidence. True, Eva had in the past cared for Nabinger, Clift, Shumway and Hanover like a mother hen protecting her brood. However, on a "what have you done for me lately" basis, she had by no means been honest and forthright with any of them.

Martha, the only one with whom she had discussed the plot, had actually been deceived into driving the death car. She also had been lied to about the amount of insurance involved so that she could later be shortchanged in the payoff. On top of this, all (except Hanover) must have had some misgivings about the purpose behind Eva's carrying policies on each of their lives.

By August 15, The full panel of jurymen were seated, ready to hear evidence. Coo, well dressed, confident and showing no outward sign of worry, sat with her attorneys. Byard routinely asked that the indictment be dismissed and Heath refused.

Byard objected to having the fire insurance and the illegally obtained life insurance policies being received in evidence. His objection was also overruled.

Grant's opening remarks outlined the facts of the murder. Byard said he would prove that Eva's confession had been obtained by torture at the police station and at the re-enactment. Furthermore, he pointed out that the state's star witness was herself a self-admitted murderess, testifying in exchange for her own life.

While in the ensuing trial Grant would bring to the stand a series of knowledgeable witnesses with damaging evidence, Byard had no witnesses that could convey more than a fleeting moment of doubt. His success would depend almost entirely on his considerable skill in cross examination of the state's witnesses. Through them, he hoped to get some admissions that would substantiate his theory that Eva had found out that Harry Wright was in the last stages of a terminal disease and would soon die. Needing money, she plastered his life with insurance policies. When he died from natural causes via an internal hemorrhage, she and Martha took his body to the Scott farm where they ran over the corpse so that they could collect double indemnity.

He hammered both Nabinger and Clift unmercifully, trying to get an admission that Nabinger was behind the plot and/or participated in it, having fallen in love with Clift and that "they were trying to put that innocent women away."

When it came time for each of the "four aces" to testify, none of them showed any malice toward Eva, but neither did they make any effort to help her case. Their forthright testimony was impossible to discredit.

Clift showed particular resiliency to Byard's cross examination, always contending that she was the soldier carrying out the orders of her superior officer. After hours of relentless pounding, Byard would leave flushed and exhausted; Clift still composed and confident. At one point Byard admonished her by commenting, "You tell this like an actress on the stage." At times she even seemed to enjoy parrying with her advisory. A small sample of the skills of both the hunter and the hunted are shown in the following direct testimony:

Byard: "It was purely an accident?"

Clift: "On my part it was."

Byard: "You hadn't any intention like that?"

Clift: "I hadn't planned on running over him. I was going to stop and Eva motioned me on."

Byard: "You're here as a self-confessed murderess. You're getting paid to testify against Eva?"

Clift: "No."

Byard: "You're getting paid with your life."

Clift: "I am telling the truth."

Byard: "You know what the penalty is for first degree murder?"

Clift: "Yes."

Byard: "You know it's burning don't you?"

Clift: "Yes."

Byard: "You know they'll roast you alive?"

Clift: "Yes."

Byard: "When you were thinking of getting roasted alive and the district attorney came with a proposition to save your life, you were agree able to it, weren't you?"

Clift: "I'm telling the truth."

Byard: "What is the difference between the story you tell now and your first story?"

Clift: "This is the truth. The other was a lie."

Byard: "In what particulars do they differ?"

Clift: "In the first story I said Eva was running the car instead of me and I said she took the car and went on driving while I went into the woods."

Byard: "Who was to know the difference if you stuck to your first story—you might be out enjoying the free air instead of facing a life in prison."

Clift: "I wanted to be fair with Eva. I'm taking my part."

Nabinger, deliberate and unhurried, also stood up under hours of unmerciful and scornful cross examination. Never did he show any sign of emotion.

Hanover and Shumway presented testimony that implicated Coo and Byard's cross examination was to discredit it rather than to implicate them. Likewise, their time on the stand was far less than for Clift and Nabinger.

Hanover played her role as a pretty airhead, exhibiting her considerable physical charms and giggling frequently during the examination. Only Shumway broke down and cried, at which point Byard bellowed, "I have no sympathy for you, young girl," to which she replied, "I didn't ask for any."

After leaving the stand, she was hysterical.

On August 27, Byard asked for a mistrial based on a remark by the district attorney and Heath denied his motion.

On August 28, protected by an agreement between the attorneys and approved by the judge, Eva testified about the conditions under which she signed her confession. She spoke in low, pleasing tones; at times her voice quivered; at times it sneered, so that far more struck the ear than was conveyed by the written record of the stenographer's flying pen. While not charging physical abuse, she claimed that she was not allowed to sleep and that Grant had offered her "consideration for the truth." Three hours of cross examination didn't change her story, but a parade of police and sheriff personnel contradicted every detail. At one point, Grant swore himself in as one of the witnesses.

On August 29, Judge Heath had to give in to an attack of influenza which also had affected a juryman and Coo herself. Testimony ceased.

On September 1st, Byard received a letter from Mrs. Charles Streeman, an Oswego society matron and crusader in the matter of women's rights, particularly among the oppressed. She had been instrumental in getting an acquittal for "Red Lilac" Jimmaron, an Indian maid from Buffalo who had been accused of murdering Mrs. Fredrick March. She now offered financial and moral support for Eva. Yet this, like other rays of hope, was quickly extinguished and she was not heard from again.

By Monday, September 3, Heath was back in action even though it was Labor Day, telling the court that he felt certain they had been less anxious about the resumption of the case than he had been. On this day, Coo's confession was admitted in evidence over Byard's objection. He argued that Coo had been illegally held from June 18 to June 21, without charges, on the pretext that she was wanted at the inquest, and so her confession was illegally obtained.

Later, in his charge to the jury, Heath said, "Now something has been said here to the effect that the so called confession may not be received because the arrest of the defendant was illegal; that she was held too long before arraignment. The proper reception of a confession does not depend necessarily upon whether the arrest was legal. The test is 'was the confession given voluntarily without the use of threats, duress, or fear, or promise of immunity from the district attorney'."

On September 4, Grant completed his case. Byard asked for dismissal for lack of evidence and the immediate arraignment of Clift. These motions were denied. He gave a long list of objections and these too were overruled. At this point, he brought the first of his seventeen witnesses to the stand; the rest appeared on the following day. There had been a short period of time on June 14 when Nabinger had not been observed in the bars and Byard contended that during the period he could have been at or near the murder scene. The testimony presented by his witnesses was intended to substantiate this theory. While this could have muddied the waters and created "reasonable doubt" in the minds of the jurors, it didn't even create a ripple.

Later, testimony was introduced to show that it was 1,114 feet (about one quarter of a mile) crosslots between the Zindle residence and the Scott house. Harry Zindle, during his testimony, was shown a picture of the Scott house taken from his home.

"Can you see the Scott residence plainly from your window where that was taken?" Byard inquired. "You can see the upper part of the house; you can see the driveway," Zindle replied.

His wife, Lucy, later testified that she was home with two of her children on June 24 and observed two people, each wearing a white shirt, in the driveway.

"What did you say to me?" Byard asked?

"I took them to be men; that is what I thought," she replied.

"You told me that you saw two men over there?"

"That is what I will believe all my life."

Upon cross examination, Grant asked, "But you don't know?"

"I don't know," was her reply.

At this point, Eva must have realized the hopelessness of her case, yet even so, she was visibly shocked and alarmed as her counsel closed what one reporter called "his amazingly brief but adroitly executed case."

THE WITNESSES

The events that preceded, occurred during, and immediately after the murder have already been narrated based on evidence given by witnesses during the trial. There is no need to repeat them here. However, this report would not be complete without giving the names of those who testified and briefly list the more important testimony they offered. Some of these people were brought to the stand on several different occasions, but their name is listed only once. Likewise, most of them were examined regarding several aspects of the case, but only the most important are listed.

For the Prosecution:

LAVINA M. SIMMONS, cousin of Wright: Testified he was born in 1880.
HERMAN SEXTON: Identified Wright in a school picture.
MYRTLE FREDERICK: Identified Wright in a school picture.
HARRY PACKARD: Identified Wright in a school picture.
WALTER BEACH, Milford Town Clerk: Wright was born before 1882, when birth records were first kept.
FREDERICK C. BURDICK: Deed to Wright's cemetery plot.
R. V. TILLAPAUGH: Wright's operating license showed birth 1880, also condition of body, burial, reenactment.
MATIE MORTON: Briefly boarded Wright.
FORD McLAURY: Wright's character.
FRED L. PLATT: Wright's inheritance in the Milford bank dwindled.
MELVIN C. BUNDY: Wright's inheritance in the Cooperstown National Bank dwindled.
MILTON B. SHEPARD: Coo accompanied Wright during Cooperstown bank withdrawals.
PERRY BENNETT: Insured Wright's Portlandville house against fire.
FRANK B. SHIPMAN: Paid Wright $350 fire insurance claim. Coo was present when it was paid.
WILBUR PORTIUS: Bought the Portlandville lot from Wright and Coo after the fire.
RAY C. ROSE, Public Welfare Commissioner: Coo asked more welfare payments for Wright.
ERNEST RUSS, Schenevus Supervisor: Coo asked higher welfare payments for Wright.
GEORGE P. HOUGHTON, Tax Collector: Coo owed taxes on Maryland

property.

ERNEST MAYNARD, State Trooper: Broke into Coo's home to get insurance policies, Coo's confession, various other evidence.

KENNETH KNAPP, State Trooper: Getting insurance policies from Coo's home, described Wright's body by road, mallet, Coo's confession, other evidence.

ROBERT J. SMITH: Coo owed taxes on Maryland property.

CHARLES C. BAUDISH: Coo owed taxes on Oneonta property.

OWEN P. BRADY, Undersheriff: Reenactment, interrogation, investigation.

JOSEPH P. MITCHELL, Deputy Sheriff: June 19 trip to Coo residence.

ROSCOE C. WHEAT, Prudential Insurance Agent: Insurance policies on Wright including one where the date of birth was changed.

ADDIE DOYLE, Mother of Edna Hanover: Introduced Metropolitan Insurance Agent to Coo.

DEWEY BUCK, Metropolitan Agent: Two insurance policies on Wright.

DR. BARNEY W. PHILLIPS: Examined Wright for Coo. Unfavorable report never sent to insurance company and he was never paid.

EARL AMES, Metropolitan Agent: Three insurance policies on Wright's life, call to settle claims.

D.D. WOODWORTH, American Agriculturist Insurance field manager: Two insurance policies on Wright.

HERBERT V. BERNARD: Approached by Coo for insurance, never followed up.

ALBERT V. BELL, Insurance agent: Asked by Shumway to stop at Coo's regarding insurance but never did.

JAMES MENSCHING, Oneonta National Aid Insurance Society: Wrote policy on Wright's life.

HARRY NABINGER: Wrote letters soliciting insurance, Decoration Day rehearsal, other trips with Coo, whereabouts on day of murder.

EDWIN R. CAMPBELL, Attorney: Wrote Wright's will; Coo was present.

ARTHUR STANLEY: Changed Wright's birth date on monument.

NELLIE SPERRY: Coo asked her to give message to Stanley.

HELEN TRUAX: Coo asked her to give message to Stanley.

WILLIAM WARNKEN, professional photographer: His photos of reenactment, Scott farm house and Woodbine Inn.

MRS. GLADYS SHUMWAY: Coo hated Wright, alibi for Clift, rehearsal.

FRED TICE, Maryland Postmaster: Described Crumhorn and its abandoned farms.

MORRIS PEAK: Made arrangements with Coo to let Clift take the Willys Knight car.

HARRY CLEMENT: Demonstrated a new Pontiac to Coo on June 13.

DWIGHT POTTER, Peak's mechanic: Let Clift take the Willys Knight.

MRS. IVA FINK: Described confrontation with Coo and Clift.

MARTH CLIFT: Her part in murder, claimed she only followed orders.

MRS. CLARA HUNT: Described confrontation with Clift and Coo.

BENJAMIN HUNT: Saw Coo and Clift at Scott house on June 14.

BENJAMIN FINK: Identified his mallet and said it was moved on Decoration Day.

MRS. CLARA MEYERS: Coo asked for alibi.

FRED PALMER: Events of June 14 including not finding Coo home, retrieving Nabinger, Coo's relations with Wright, Coo's asking alibi.

EDNA HANOVER: Coo's relations with Wright, retrieving Nabinger on June 14, being silenced by Coo regarding amount of insurance.

DR. JAMES T. GREENOUGH, Coroner: Wright could not have been killed by a hit and run driver.

JAMES JOHNSON: Did not see Coo, Nabinger or Wright on June 14.

GEORGE MICHERLEIN, Proprietor of Pop's Inn: Did not see Coo, Nabinger, or Wright on June 14.

EDITH (PEGGY) PARSONS, employee of Pop's Inn: Did not see Coo, Nabinger, or Wright on June 14.

DR. NORMAN D. GETMAN, Otsego County Coroner: Reenactment, coroner's inquest.

DR. CARL WINSOR, Acting Coroner: Condition of Wright's body.

EVA COO (Appeared with prosecution witnesses): Conditions under which she signed confession.

DONALD GRANT, District Attorney: Coo not promised immunity.

AUBREY WHITNEY, State Trooper: Coo's treatment at time of confession.

GEORGE MITCHELL, Sheriff: The investigation, evidence, arraignment, coroner's inquest, reenactment, treatment during questioning.

RALPH HANNER, State Trooper: Regarding Coo's questioning.

LOUIS FRIER, State Trooper: Regarding Coo's questioning.

SGT. JOHN (JACK) CUNNINGHAM, State Trooper: Regarding Coo's questioning.

WILLIAM E. CADWELL, State Trooper: Wright's body beside the road, interrogation.

CPL. ROY ZIEMAN, State Trooper: Coo's statement.

DERMONT R. KEOWN, State Trooper: Coo's Statement.

JOHN M. HOTALING, Attorney: Coo's statement.

CHARLES SISSON, Peak's mechanic: Identified photo of Wills Knight car.

DR. HARRY L. CRUTTENDEN: Need for sleep.

SGT. JOSEPH A. MURPHY: Coo's statement.

ROBERT D. HANNAHS, Deputy Sheriff: Investigation.

HAROLD D. CARPENTER, Justice of the peace: Coo's arraignment.

For the Defense

STANLEY FELTER, Professional photographer: His photographs of Scott farmhouse, Woodbine Inn taken for the defense.

HARRY ZINDLE: Saw unknown people on Decoration Day, told Hunt and Fink, found mallet on porch and returned it to the house.

CLIFFORD OLMSTEAD: Believed that it was Nabinger who "tooted his horn" in passing his home in Cooperstown Junction between 7:30 and 8 p.m. on June 14.

MRS. HELENA OLMSTEAD: Corroborated her husband's statement.

WILLIAM TARBOX, co-owner of Alpine Restaurant: Nabinger at the bar on June 14 at 10:30 p.m.

EDWARD MEAD, Alpine Restaurant employee: Nabinger at bar between 10:15 and 10:30 p.m.

ELLIS KROEHN: Nabinger in Alpine Restaurant on June 14.

DR. HARRY CRUTTENDEN: Wright's body exhumed Aug. 11 was too decomposed to examine for bruises.

LYNN G. PARSHALL: Identified a map of Coo and Meyers property.

JAMES PERRY, Manager of Alpine Restaurant: Saw Nabinger come in between 10:15 and 10:30 and leave at 12:45 a.m.

HENRY CROSS, Oneonta Police Officer: On June 24, he took a mallet from Scott house as a souvenir.

MELVIN THOMAS: On June 19, he picked up a mallet at Scott house and gave it to investigators.

LUCY (MRS. HARRY) ZINDLE: Saw two people at Scott farm house at time of murder.

CHARLES CHOATE: Drove Nabinger in his taxi to South Side to see Clift on June 15.

GEORGE NOBLE, Proprietor of Noble's Restaurant: Nabinger there on June 14 between noon and 1 p.m., left between 5 and 6 p.m., back at 9 p.m.

JOHN (JACK) SWARTZ: Worked in the garage that had repossessed Clift's

Dodge due to discrepancy in signature on note.
DR. GEORGE W. AUGUSTINE: Condition of Wright's body when
exhumed on Aug.11, and need for sleep.

Note: The spelling of the names varies widely in different accounts, particularly in newspaper articles. The list above uses spelling found in the official
records in the Otsego County Clerk's office.

THE VERDICT

When court again convened on September 6, Byard's summation lasted
for seventy-eight minutes. In it, he portrayed Coo as betrayed by her friends,
her lover and the law. For the next 100 minutes, Grant's summation described
her as a "tiger women." After Heath's forty-five minute charge to the jury,
Eva's fate was in the hands of twelve farmers.

She awaited the verdict in the now famous Kilkenny office, the very
room where the defense contended she had received non-stop questioning
until she finally agreed to sign a confession in exchange for an opportunity
to rest. There, amiable and cheerful, she now readily talked with reporters,
answered their questions, and graciously posed with Byard for photogra-
phers.

After only two hours of deliberation, the jury reached a verdict. The court
had not expected such speedy justice and when the word spread, a capacity
crowd jammed into the courtroom. Coo trembled visibly as she walked into
the chamber, supported by Byard. She was met by hisses and boos from
women in the crowd while Heath repeatedly rapped his gavel, called for
order, and threatened to clear the room of spectators.

As order was restored, chaos reverted to utter silence broken only by the
judge's query, "Gentlemen, have you reached a verdict?"

Mr. Ainslie, acting as foreman, replied, "Our verdict is guilty as
charged."

After the judge asked for clarification, he said, "Guilty of murder first
degree."

Again, chaos reigned in the courtroom. Eva, tears streaming down her
cheeks, trembled visibly, cheers and loud applause from her tormentors ring-
ing in her ears. Heath rebuked the onlookers and again called for order.

As soon as silence was restored, Eva, now in control of her emotions, set her stern face and turned toward the court.

"Your peers have found you guilty of murdering Harry Wright on Crumhorn Mountain the night of June 14," he said. "The law says you must die. I sentence you to die in the manner and method prescribed by the state of New York—electrocution in the electric chair at Sing Sing. I commit you to the custody of Sheriff Mitchell who must deliver you to Sing Sing within ten days and I sentence you to die the week of October 15. May God have mercy on your soul."

Twenty minutes later, he passed sentence on Clift who, through her attorney, had pleaded guilty to second degree murder. As per the plea bargained agreement, she was sentenced to serve "not less than twenty years or more than life" in Bedford Hills Prison For Women. Martha, head bowed, wept softly, dabbing at her eyes with her hankerchief as she heard her fate.

Immediately upon hearing Coo's sentence, Byard moved that the verdict be set aside and a new trial granted. Heath allowed him five days in which to submit his motion in writing.

As the *Oneonta Daily Star* observed, "In practically every case appeals are taken in first degree murder convictions. It is thought that if the request for a new trial is denied, a certificate of reasonable doubt will be sought from Justice Heath, which is necessary for an appeal. It is almost always customary to grant such a certificate to allow an appeal. In such cases, the appeal goes direct to the Court of Appeals and not the Appellate division."

In addressing the spectators after the defendants had been sentenced and had left the courtroom, Justice Heath said that unquestionably the Coo trial would be remembered, but the operation of the court would be forgotten. Yet history has not seen it that way.

Heath commended Grant for his expertise, particularly in enlisting Martha, saying, "It was quite evident that unless someone had opened up on what took place on Crumhorn Mountain, there would never have been any trial."

After expanding on this statement, he continued, "I want to say to the district attorney that his conduct in not giving absolute immunity was very commendable. It took some nerve to take such a position and go through with it. It is for that reason that Martha Clift is facing a sentence that is some sentence, instead of going scot free."

Coo, on the other hand, had no kind words for Grant. However, when asked about the judges conduct she said that "Judge Heath (was) very fair."

As for Byard, she still had confidence that he would eventually extricate her from her predicament. "I know you'll get me out," she told him.

OTSEGO'S DISGRACE

The trial had produced 2,268 pages of testimony and cost the county $12,500. Seventy-four witnesses had appeared for the state and seventeen for the defense, crowded into a period that lasted only eighteen days (three of which were consumed in selecting the jury). Those sessions included one on a Saturday and one on a legal holiday (Labor Day). Heath had repeatedly threatened to hold night sessions if it was necessary in order to speed up the proceedings.

The investigation and trial had speedily purged prim and proper Otsego County of its embarrassment. Therefore, it should come as no surprise that on the morning of September 7, only a few hours after hearing the verdict and sentence, the disgrace was sent down to Ossining for final disposal. In fact, there was such haste that no one remembered to tell the people at Sing Sing that they were to have guests that day.

Both Coo and Clift left their cells dressed in their most colorful finery. Each realized that they would be destined to wear dull, drab prison uniforms for many years, if not for the rest of their lives.

In front of the jail, two cars lined up, one a sedan with Deputy Joseph Mitchell at the wheel; the other car was manned by Sheriff George Mitchell. As Coo, her pale blue eyes misty with tears, stepped out of her cell, she remonstrated with a photographer, "Do you have to do that?"

As she passed Nabinger's cell, she stopped briefly to hand him a photograph that showed her surrounded by news people. "Here's something I like a lot," she said, pressing the print into his outstretched hand.

Nabinger, sad-eyed and pale, clenched the print and swallowed hard, but the lips that had betrayed her during the trial were now silent.

As Clift and Coo met in front of the jail, they tenderly embraced and kissed each other goodbye. As Coo stepped into the car driven by Deputy Joseph Mitchell, she called out to Clift, "I'll remember you as long as I live."

Clift climbed into the sedan piloted by Sheriff Mitchell, and after Dorothy Kilgallen, a news correspondent and Ray Howard, a news photographer climbed aboard, the car pulled away from the curb.

Mrs. George Mitchell, Jim Byard and Owen P. Brady joined Coo and Deputy Joseph Mitchell in the second car. As they left, Shumway and

Hanover were softly weeping in their upstairs cells.

The somber caravan was little more than out of sight before Nabinger, Hanover, and Shumway were set free. The state no longer required their services.

As Otsego County's disposal units merged into traffic near the prison, a macabre twist occurred. A hearse, there to receive the remains of Alphonse Brengard, a recently electrocuted prisoner, accidentally joined the procession directly behind the car that carried Eva. Her glance roved over the outlines of the glassed-in limousine, as this harbinger of doom doggedly followed her to the prison gates.

Now the little group reorganized. After Coo and Clift said their final farewells, Deputy Joseph Mitchell drove away with Clift enroute to nearby Bedford Hills Prison For Women. As the *New York Daily News* not so delicately put it, " 'Tattletale Martha' to enter prison, her 20 pieces of silver for playing Judas (to) be 20 years in Bedford Reformatory."

The others moved on toward Sing Sing's reception center.

As the hunters arrived with their trophy, they did not receive the acclaim they had anticipated. Warden Lewis E. Lawes was away on vacation in Bermuda and John Sheeby, acting warden and Flen Ferling, the warden's secretary were in charge.

Eva was ushered into a room where she gave up her remaining possessions—two five-and-dime necklaces, a big ring that may or may not have held a diamond, and $5.75 in cash. After being given prison garb, she was escorted into a cell recently vacated by Mrs. Anna Antonio who had killed her husband for his insurance money, and before that by Ruth Snyder who with her lover had killed her husband. Both had died in the chair.

One of the first things that Eva asked was, "Say, what kind of a place is Sing Sing anyway?" In an effort to reassure her, the matron replied, "Oh, it's not a bad place; Warden Lawes is a fine man and Mrs. Lawes is very kind to women prisoners. Do you know what they did for Mrs. Antonio?"

Eva cut her off. "Yeah . . . burned her," she snapped.

Dr. James Kearney found the prisoner to be in good health and her only complaint seemed to be that she was denied cosmetics and peroxide for her hair. She was in reasonably good spirits, knowing that back in Oneonta, her attorneys were busy in her behalf.

Otsego County had by now agreed to pay Holmes and Byard another $1,000 to further represent her and so on September 11, they formally filed a notice of appeal with the Court of Appeals and on the 12th, served a notice of appeal to Donald H. Grant. They also formally filed briefs with Justice Riley H. Heath, asking that the jury's verdict of guilty be set aside on the grounds of insufficient evidence and other points and asked for a new trial. By filing the notice of appeal, the execution set for the week of October 15 was automatically postponed until the case could be argued and settled.

It was pointed out that a stenographer would need a month to transcribe the 3,000 folios if he worked steadily, and he had other duties which would make it impossible to complete the records of the trial and have them printed (as required by law), by the time that the Court of Appeals would convene on October 1. It was also expected that it would take the court another nine weeks to review and act upon the case.

Attorneys traditionally use time and delays to the benefit of their clients. Therefore one must be curious if not suspicious as to why "Mr. Holmes stated yesterday that the defense would do without transcriptions of certain portions of the evidence in order to hasten the appeal," as was revealed by a newspaper item on September 13.

SING SING

In the meantime, Sheriff and Mrs. Mitchell were hopping mad. The sheriff had done a commendable job in carrying out his duties and the press had bathed him in well deserved adoration. He had learned to savor fame, but his role in bringing Eva to justice had not been recognized in Ossining.

Mitchell fired off the following letter:

Warden Lewis E. Lawes
Ossining, N.Y.

Dear Warden Lawes:
It is with regret that after my first visit to your institution I am forced to write this letter to you. Yesterday, September 7th, when I delivered Eva Coo to the Sing Sing prison, after entering the front door of the prison, I introduced myself, Mrs. Mitchell, matron, Undersheriff Owen P. Brady and James J. Byard, Jr., attorney for Mrs. Coo.

After hearing and reading of the wonderful treatment accorded to prisoners in your institution, I was amazed and horrified to have Mrs. Coo, my prisoner, as I had not yet turned the papers over to anyone, nor had I been asked to do so , rudely snatched from my hands and shoved into another room and had the door of that room closed in our faces.

Mrs. Mitchell, my wife, who is the matron of the Otsego County jail, asked if she could not say goodbye to Mrs. Coo, and she was told that she had seen her for the last time, and all of us were told to 'get out.' This, too, was before any commitment papers had been asked for. I replied that I would leave when I got a receipt for my prisoner, and was informed that I could go upstairs and I would be taken care of there, no one even offering to show me the way.

After finding the office myself, I left the commitment papers and received a receipt for my prisoner.

In the meantime, Undersheriff Brady and Attorney Byard, who were standing outside prison bars, were asked about Mrs. Coo's baggage. Undersheriff Brady and Attorney Byard re-entered the prison to help look for this grip which no one seemed to know anything about after it had been left in their care. On their return they were greeted by Principal Keeper Sheehy, for whose gentlemanly conduct Undersheriff Brady and Attorney Byard can express only appreciation.

Now, warden, this is to inform you I am ready to prefer charges against one whom I am informed is called Flen Ferling and the guards and others who were on duty at that period in your prison. I will await your reply before further action.

I am sending a copy of this letter to the Hon. Walter E. Thayer, chairman of the State Commission of Correction, State Office Building, Albany, New York.

Very respectfully,
George H. Mitchell,
Sheriff of Otsego County

After mailing the letter to Lawes as well as Lawes' boss, he called together a news conference and gave each correspondent a copy of the letter. Not letting the matter stop there, he expanded upon it. He said that being acquainted with the nationwide reputation which Warden Lawes had attained as an expert in dealing with crime and criminals, and having also read the warden's book on life in Sing Sing, he had expected to find the prison a model where conditions were exemplary.

He expressed surprise at the reception of his prisoner, while the treatment accorded him and his deputies was such as to lead him to believe that formal charges were perfectly justified. Both Sheriff Mitchell and Undersheriff Brady did not hesitate to state that they believed that the guards and others whom they contacted were all under the influence of intoxicating liquor.

They said that Attorney Byard might even have secured Coo's release, had he been so inclined, due to the conduct of the prison guards, on the grounds that she was being improperly held. He added that it was his understanding that Byard had also registered a formal complaint to the officials.

To understand Lawes' reaction, one must remember that he had a very large ego, regularly cultivated and fertilized by his associates in the field of criminology. Furthermore, he had a reputation to uphold. Ask anyone on the street at the time as to the greatest authority on crime and punishment and three names would be heard: God Almighty, of the Universe; J. Edgar Hoover, of the Federal Bureau of Investigation; and Warden Lewis E. Lawes, of Sing Sing, but not necessarily in that order.

Lawes had not only lectured and written books on the subject but he was revered on such popular shows as "Gangbusters." Reputedly, his prison was the model and other wardens would do well to imitate his methods, but should never expect to reach Sing Sing's standards of excellence.

Furthermore, while commissioned to execute many of his guests, he did not personally believe in capital punishment and Eva was to be with him for a short stay on death row. It is not surprising that he greeted this missile of blasphemy from what he considered an upstart country sheriff with the same disdain and contempt that he would have for a mosquito that briefly settled on his arm for a blood sample. On September 19, Mitchell received his reply.

> I have very carefully looked into the matter mentioned in your letter," the warden wrote, "relative to Mrs. Coo and while there may have appeared to have been some abruptness here when you delivered the prisoner, you must understand that we receive about 4,500 prisoners during the year and there are certain rules laid down as a receiving procedure.
>
> If I were here I might have acted differently. I don't know. In the meantime after carefully looking into the matter there seems to be no cause for any charges and I am rather surprised you gave your letter to the newspapers, which seems rather discourteous to me.
>
> Certainly we treat the inmate with courtesy and have no desire to extend any other treatment to visiting officials or the public in general.
>
> I am attaching herewith copies of the reports of the officers interested.

Reports of the arrival of Mrs. Coo by Principal Keeper John Sheehy and the warden's secretary, Flen Ferling were attached to the letter.

What had promised to be a battle of egos turned out to be a minor scourmish. David had met Goliath—but his pebble only ricocheted off his foe's armour. Yet Mitchell would not forgive nor forget. His motto would be, "Don't get mad; get even."

LAWES SWATS ANTAGONIST NUMBER TWO

Hundreds of newspapers all across the United States and Canada continued to clamor for more news about Eva. Overseas, the *Daily Telegram of London*, The *Chicago Tribune's* daily Paris edition, and the *Herald Tribune's* European edition were among several overseas editions of the United States papers that carried the accounts. Foreign language newspapers included *Corriere d' America* (Italian), *National Herald* (Greek), and *La Presse* (French). While home town newspapers might be satisfied with what Eva was served for dinner, the larger ones wanted something with more meat.

Yet news items were now very hard to obtain. Rules barred Eva from talking with reporters so they had to rely on what they could get from guards, matrons, and if they were lucky, from the warden.

Eva remained in good humor. Sometimes it appeared that she was actually taunting death. When she mailed a letter, she was required to add her prisoner identification number. Below it, she added, "Don't think this is my phone number."

Her favorite one-liner was, "Some of my friends outside complain they find it difficult to get into Sing Sing. I didn't have any trouble." That was a bitter half truth. It was very difficult to get in to visit Eva, but if Eva had friends left, they were not trying to break down the bars to see her. In fact, her only callers had been Jim Byard, accompanied by "a secretary," there to try to save her skin, and both a Protestant and Catholic chaplain, there to try to salvage her soul. Each came as a matter of duty rather than friendship.

In mid-September she applied for tickets to see a series of football games that the inmates played within the prison walls, but because her address was on death row, her request was denied. She would have to listen to the game alone, on the radio.

The staff treated Eva kindly but to a person who had spent a lifetime surrounded by boisterous friends and patrons, the isolation and total lack of company was beginning to take its toll. Yet she kept up her spirits knowing that back in Oneonta, Sunny Jim was hard at work, preparing the papers for her appeal . . . the papers that would set her free or if not that, then reduce the sentence to the same one that friend Martha was serving at Bedford Hills.

While the court stenographer, Herbert H. Sterling, and his two secretaries were busily transcribing the notes from the trial, October 18, the original date for the execution came and went as did the Court of Appeals' October session. On October 29, the 2,268 pages of court records were ready to be printed.

On that date, the *Oneonta Daily Star* quoted Byard as saying that "a case was recently decided by the Court of Appeals in which a new trial was ordered for a witness who was kept over thirty-six hours without arraignment before a magistrate." He believed that on that point alone, a new trial would be granted. He said he was ready to argue the case as soon as the printers had finished their work.

It was further stated that copies of the appeal had already been sent to Governor Lehman, Warden Lawes, Grant, Heath, and W.O. Hintermister, the county clerk, by Byard and Holmes. Byard was quoted as saying that briefs had already been prepared and would be ready as soon as references from the record were inserted. He would argue the case as soon as the Court of Appeals was in session.

In the meantime, the *New York Sunday Mirror* was featuring a sensational scoop consisting of a series of weekly articles entitled, "The Life and Good Times of Eva Coo." To add a lot of mystery and suspense to an already lurid narrative, it was said that the concluding installment would be held in a vault and would not be published until after Eva was electrocuted. The story was written under Eva's byline.

On November 10, competing newspapers had a story, leaked from the warden's fiefdom, more succulent than they could have ever envisioned. It stated that Dr. Walter N. Thayer, Jr., Commissioner of Corrections, had asked an investigation as to the author of the articles that were appearing in the *Mirror*. Dr. Thayer had requested Attorney General Bennett to conduct a hearing in New York City at which Warden Lewis E. Lawes, who had called the matter to the attention of Thayer, would be given an opportunity "to establish his innocence of violating any rules or regulations of prison administration."

Dr. Thayer was quoted as regarding the story as a reflection, not only upon the Department of Corrections and himself, but upon Warden Lawes and the entire state government. He stated that books and records would be brought before the commissioner at the hearing, at which time an attempt to find the responsible parties would be made.

Newspapers carried the item on November 10, but actually the hearing had already been held on Friday, November 9 in the State Building at 50 Center Street in New York City. Lawes had testified that on September 19 he was served with a court order to permit James J. Byard, Jr., attorney for Mrs. Coo, and John Kobler to visit Mrs. Coo to "transact certain business." Upon more recent investigation, it was determined that Mr. Kobler was a newspaper man and the articles began to appear after his visit. He contended that Byard had taken "unfair advantage" of Coo and obtained the story by "misrepresentation," and that the interview was a clear violation of the rules and regulations of the crime commission.

Mrs. Minnie Kopp, prison matron, testified that Byard introduced Kobler as a court stenographer and that they were visiting Coo to get "something good" to present to the Court of Appeals. She said they were there for four hours and that on several occasions Coo asked if the information was for the newspapers and Byard had assured her that it was only for his own personal use.

Father John P. McCaffey, chaplin, testified that Coo had told him that she had been told that Byard received $3,000 for setting up the meeting. Rev. Dr. Anthony W. Peterson, the Protestant chaplain and Joseph W. Connaughton, correspondence censor, corroborated previous testimony.

Byard not only was not there to defend himself, but in fact did not even know the meeting was in progress, according to what he later told reporters. Therefore, no one asked where Coo received her secondhand information, alleging a payoff, but with only prison personnel allowed to visit her, the answer appeared quite obvious.

A letter signed by Coo said that she was not the author of the article and that she was "greatly disturbed" by its appearance, feeling that these articles "won't help—they'll send me to the chair."

The knife was deep within Byard's reputation, but just to give it a sadistic twist, the same Flen Ferling who Mitchell, in his complaint to the same crime commissioner had claimed was drunk on the job, now had the satisfaction of adding his signature below Eva's on the line reserved for witnessing her signature.

Two days before Christmas, Byard received his present from the State Department of Corrections—a copy of their report. It was no surprise that they found the articles appearing in the *Sunday Mirror* "were not in fact written by her (Coo) and were published over her protest to the prison authorities."

Furthermore, "the Committee recommends in view of certain statements made in the course of the inquiry that the report and testimony be presented to the State Bar Association."

Not surprisingly, they also determined that "There were no violations of rules and regulations of Sing Sing prison by the warden or those of the prison staff having to do with the custody of said Eva Coo and that the advertised statements that the said article were written by Eva Coo in the death house were untrue and without foundation."

BETRAYED

All through history, men and women have gone to their deaths, devastated more by a trusted friend's betrayal than by the results of that betrayal. As Julius Caesar lamented, "Et tu, Brute" when he saw his friend draw the dagger from beneath his cloak, as Harry Wright had forced from his crushed chest a final, "Now I know why you brought me here," now too, Eva felt a pain far greater than the state could possibly exact by merely burning her body.

She had trusted her attorney and suddenly she had been told by prison personnel that he had betrayed her. She was in the big arena and with the world looking on, she had been ready to again fight for her life, but within an instant she felt that her friend had betrayed her. She was sick at heart and her general health would start to rapidly deteriorate from that moment on.

It is very doubtful that the story about her earlier life and love affairs could in itself have possibly damaged her upcoming appeal. Yet she, who had deceived Harry Wright, had now been deceived by Byard and there could be no mending of their former relationship.

This certainly did not go unnoticed by Lawes, who immediately took advantage of the opportunity. One can only speculate on whether his action was for humanitarian reasons or to be in a position to further settle the score with Mitchell and Byard.

Lawes suggested that she replace Byard with the law firm of Slade and Slade. He wanted to see Coo either go free or receive a lighter sentence on a second degree murder conviction, possibly for her own well-being and certainly to further humiliate the upstarts from the hill country. Slade and Slade had a good track record in defending people held for murder both in initial trials and appeals. By having his friends appointed to represent Coo, it would also now be possible to have them do the dirty work as his vendetta against his adversaries continued.

Taking the warden's advice, Coo wrote a long letter to Slade and Slade, a portion of which said, "I will be pleased to hear from you at a very early date as I am anxious to do something at once. I don't feel this lawyer would do justice for me at the Court of Appeals as I don't think he wants me out on account of the story he wrote. He will not come here to see me. Warden Lawes knows about my attorney so I would advise you to see him."

"After I was sent here, my lawyer wrote my life's story in the *Sunday Mirror*, which was a terrible story and I have been told he received from $3,000 to $5,000 for it."

On January 8, 1935, David Slade and Joseph N. Klein of the firm of Slade and Slade met with James J. Byard, Jr. and Everett B. Holmes before Justice Riley H. Heath of Binghamton, at which time Slade asked that Byard and Holmes be dismissed from the case and that Slade and Slade be appointed to succeed them in representing Coo and receiving her power of attorney.

There were bitter arguments between the attorneys in which Eva's welfare was completely forgotten. Slade condemned Byard for "unprofessional conduct" and "selfish interests." He said that Everett Holmes had told him that no part of the brief submission to the Court of Appeals had been prepared and that Holmes was willing to step down and offered full cooperation.

Byard pointed out that he was being persecuted only because of Mitchell's complaint about his reception at Sing Sing and he declared that he hadn't even submitted a formal complaint of his own. He also stated that ever since that incident, prison officials had been trying to persuade Coo to dismiss him and hire another attorney. He said that Slade had participated in this "underhanded" maneuver.

Byard now faced the same problems for his own well being as he had earlier faced in Eva's defense. All the evidence, all the men with power, all the money was against him. After being promised payment for the work already performed, he was willing to sign the following stipulation which Judge Heath and his associates had executed earlier that day.

"Upon the annexed consent of Eva Coo, James J. Byard, Jr. and Everett B. Holmes, consenting that Messers. Slade & Slade of 521 Fifth Ave., New York City, be and they hereby are substituted as attorneys for the defendant in the place and stead of James J. Byard, Jr. and Everett B. Holmes, present attorneys for said defendant.

. . . and it is further ordered that the substitution herein made and ordered is without any reflection as to the conduct of said former attorneys in their professional capacity.

. . . and it is further ordered that any expenses incurred by said former attorneys shall not be prejudiced by this order."

Slade asked that the Court of Appeals hearing scheduled for January 17 be extended to March 4 so that he could read the court records and prepare his case. Grant said that he would not object and the extension was granted. Now, Slade had his opportunity to show the country bumpkins how the competent, slick city attorneys got results.

Meanwhile, back in her lonely cell on death row, Eva languished, while the people commissioned to protect her fought among themselves rather than for her interests. At long last she realized her desperate plight. Prison officials said she had cracked under the strain. They told of how she had fits of hysterical weeping and one reported, "Eva is carrying on pathetically."

In fact, it can safely be said that the defiant Eva who was first apprehended, the cocky, vibrant, wise cracking, "I can take it" Eva who taunted death during the trial, and the composed, confident Eva who had entered Sing Sing had vanished. In her place was a haggard, confused, frightened and broken old woman. One quick turn of events had accomplished what no amount of interrogation, no amount of evidence, no amount of brutality had been able to achieve.

LAWES SNARES ENEMY NUMBER ONE

On February 28, Slade came up with important information that would bring about justice and obliterate any suspicion of guilt. Unfortunately, it was not for his client, Coo, but for his mentor, Lawes.

The March issue of *True Detective Mysteries* carried an article entitled "The Truth About The Eva Coo Case, as told to A. Milton Learned by Sheriff Mitchell."

Slade wrote a letter to Governor Herbert E. Lehman and sent a copy of it to Sheriff Mitchell. In it he charged that Mitchell was neglectful of his duties as a public official and asked that an investigation of the sheriff's office with the intent of removing the official from office be implemented.

The attorney charged that the story was prejudicial to their client's case and that it would be detrimental to Coo's well being when they argued her case before the Court of Appeals.

The letter went on for some length, citing paragraphs and sentences which the attorneys claimed would work to the disadvantage of their client. While laymen do not perceive solemn high court judges reading and being swayed by the accounts in pulp magazines, apparently it did concern Coo's attorneys.

On March 14, Mitchell with his attorney, Clermont G. Tennant, appeared before Charles Poletti, counsel to Governor Herbert H. Lehman, in his Albany office. In answering the charges, he submitted a prepared statement. It said that on or about September 6, Mr. Learned, city editor of the *Star*, asked the sheriff for permission to use his name in connection with an article relating to the Coo case, which Mr. Learned contemplated writing for publication in the detective magazine, saying that it was customary with such stories to use the name of a prominent police official.

After this meeting, he signed a mimeographed form furnished by the magazine giving them permission for the use of his name as telling the story to Mr. Learned "and that was his only connection with the said article in any manner."

He said that Learned was one of the newsmen who covered the case and thus became familiar with it. He did not discuss anything in connection with the story with Learned, did not see it while it was being written, or after it was completed until the magazine appeared on the news stands. He contended that the story was based on facts taken from court records.

Furthermore, he stated

" . . . that no consideration, financial or otherwise, was ever offered to respondent for the use of his name in connection with the article and that respondent had never received any consideration from *True Detective Mysteries* or from any other person or persons and did not, and does not, expect to receive any consideration therefor."

The statement further declared,

"Respondent denies all of the acts of misconduct in said charges set forth, and denies that he ever violated his oath of office.

"Respondent denies the commission of any act prejudicial to the case of the said Eva Coo or that he ever disclosed any confidential matter imparted to him as alleged in said charges.

"Respondent denies that the publication of the said article in *True Detective Mysteries* was in violation of his oath of office as sheriff.

"Respondent denies that he ever wrote the heading of said article as quoted in said charges or had any knowledge as to how the said article was to be titled or headed and respondent denies that he ever wrote the portions of the said articles as quoted in the charges herein or had any knowledge in reference to same and knew nothing about said quotations until he read same in the March issue of *True Detective Mysteries*.

"Respondent denies that he told any portion of the story . . . purportedly to have been told to the said A. Milton Learned, or to any other person."

Accompanying the sheriff's answer was an affidavit made by Mr. Learned in which he substantiated Mitchell's statements.

SLADE STRUCK OUT

After pouring over 2,109 pages of court records, Slade submitted a 116 page brief to the Court of Appeals and sent a copy to Grant.

Nine points were made describing why the murder conviction should be reversed. It was said that no murder actually occurred because Wright died by accident, that the confession was obtained by threats, duress, intimidation and torture. Coo could not have entered the Scott house and secured the mallet because the door was locked, and if she did enter, how could she have locked it after leaving?

Slade contended that the mallet was a "plant" selected from several that were available. He questioned Nabinger's whereabouts between the hours of 6 and 9 p.m. Coo could not have received a fair trial in Otsego County so a change of venue should have been granted. He called the "coroner's evidence incompetent" in which a "reversible error was committed." The jury heard Coo's confession during the inquest even though it was later declared inadmissible. The court should not have allowed the evidence on Wright's physical condition or Coo's treatment of him. The court should not have admitted illegally taken evidence. Grant's conduct in questioning and in summation had been inflammatory, incompetent and unwarranted. He said that none of the charges made during the trial had been proven beyond a reasonable doubt.

Each and every one of the charges had been skillfully argued by Byard in the initial trial and Heath had shot them down. Slade's hope was that the Appeals Court would find that the judge had erred in one or more of these decisions.

The case was argued in Albany beginning on March 4. On April 29, the court rendered it's verdict.

"No error was committed by the trial judge in denying defendant's motion for a change in venue.
"The evidence admitted contained every necessary element of the

crime of murder first degree.

"Any statements made by the defendant and received in evidence were properly admitted.

"The statements and admissions of the defendant are sufficiently corroborated under the rules of confession to warrant a conviction of the crime charged.

"No error was committed in respect to defendant's statement made in the presence of the coroner during the evening of June 22-23.

"The testimony of the accomplice, Martha Clift, is sufficiently corroborated by the testimony of numerous other witnesses.

"There was a legal and relevant purpose in introducing evidence both that Harry Wright was addicted to the excessive use of liquor, was physically weak, and was a semi-cripple and that the defendant frequently abused him and locked him in or out of the house when she went away therefrom.

"The fact that some of the people's witnesses were recalled and that the district attorney at times asked leading questions was not prejudicial to the defendant.

"The district attorney's summation was both just and fair to the defendant and no-where contains improper references.

"No error was committed by the trial judge in charging the jury."

In this manner, all of the other objections, too, were dismissed. The fatal conclusion stated, "People, respondent, versus Eva Coo, appellant: judgement of conviction affirmed. No opinion. All concur."

Lawes wrote a note to Coo and Sheehy delivered it to her. "What do you think? I've been turned down," was her only comment.

Grant praised Heath saying that he " . . . saved the county the expense of another trial . . . so well versed in the law, that there could be no reversal." Of Byard, he said that with the limited evidence available to him, no attorney could have presented a better case.

The death warrant, a printed form with the blank space for the inscription of the names and dates, was completed to read, "It is ordered and adjudged that the week beginning Monday the 24th of June in the year of our Lord one thousand nine hundred and thirty-five be and the same hereby is fixed as the week during which original sentence of death shall be executed upon the defendant herein." On May 1, all seven Appeal Court judges signed it. Inasmuch as all executions occurred on Thursday, that meant that unless the Governor intervened, Eva would die on June 27.

The Governor set June 19 as the date on which he would review the petition for executive clemency for both Patrick Downey, convicted of murdering nine-year-old Rita Lazzari, and Eva Coo, convicted of murdering Harry Wright. At 2 p.m., Slade would represent Coo, and Grant would speak for the people.

Back in Sing Sing, Coo was no longer exercising. She was becoming thin and wasted, her appetite gone and she could seldom sleep. June 26 marked her 43rd birthday and Mrs. Lawes and the other women at the prison prepared a chicken dinner and a birthday cake. Ironically, the date also celebrated the first anniversary of Harry Wright's burial and Eva's being taken into custody. It was that first anniverary that now negated any cheer from the "Happy Birthday" etched in pink icing across the cake's frosting.

She still held on to one faint hope that the governor might commute her sentence to life imprisonment. This was nutured by a disclosure, now for the first time revealed by Mary Warner, a native of Windsor and friend of both Coo and Clift. It was very unusual for death row prisoners to be allowed to host visitors, but Supreme Court Justice Arthur S. Tompkins of Nyack had signed an order that allowed Mrs. Warner to visit Coo on May 20. She was allowed to call on Clift a few days later.

In her signed affidavit, Warner claimed that Clift had received a visitor who introduced himself as the Governor of New York State while she was awaiting trial in Cooperstown. This man promised her that if she would testify against Eva, he would pardon her immediately after Eva's electrocution.

Byard had previously failed to convince a judge and jury in the initial trial with reasonable arguments, and Slade using substantially the same reasoning, had already failed to convince the panel of judges on the Court of Appeals. Slade dropped the twice-failed arguments and came up with a radically new script for the Governor's consideration on June 19.

Now Slade claimed that Coo had been "improperly defended" at her trial because she was refused the right to tell her own story and he asked the Governor to make a "complete investigation" of the proceedings.

David, the eldest Slade, shouted so loudly that his voice could be heard outside of the huge executive chamber as he came up with a revised account of the events of June 14. After having languished behind Sing Sing's bars for several months, Eva had remembered some major errors in her prior confessions and Slade repeated to the Governor her latest version of what happened on the day that Wright died, as he had "received it from her own lips."

On the morning of June 14, Martha had motored up to Woodbine Inn, driving a car she hoped to buy. She asked Eva if she would like to go for a ride and as Eva needed groceries, she agreed to go with Clift. They went to

Worcester where Eva bought provisions while Martha caroused in the local tavern with a couple of her gentlemen friends. After that, they returned to Eva's home.

Harry Wright was atop a ladder, painting the inn and as Martha entered the driveway, the car accidentally hit the ladder, causing Harry to fall to the ground.

As Slade pointed out, "Mrs. Coo, with that big hearted nature that characterizes those of the hillbilly country, rushed to the aid of the fallen Wright. Having been a nurse, she realized that Wright was badly injured or dead. She wanted to call the troopers or a doctor but Mrs. Clift pleaded with her that she was in enough trouble already and persuaded Mrs. Coo not to summon outsiders."

Otsego County residents would bristle at being called hillbillies but to lump them in with "big hearted" Eva, whom they had deported, was really rubbing it in. Given the opportunity, they would have pointed out that Eva, a woman of the world, had formerly lived in New York City where she might have picked up her bad habits.

The two women put the body in the car and went for a ride on Crumhorn Mountain, seeking a way out of their delemma. As they reached a point near the Scott farm, Martha became faint. The party entered the driveway "so Martha could rest up and calm her nerves." Coo was quoted as saying, "I had to fan her to revive her."

While there, Mr. and Mrs. Hunt arrived and a confrontation took place. Mrs. Hunt searched the machine with a flashlight furnished by Mrs. Coo and then departed.

"Within a half minute, Mrs. Coo followed them. "How could they have gotten the body out of its hiding place and into the car and departed within a half-minute of the time the car left?" Slade asked.

Martha drove directly to Woodbine Inn and after leaving her, "drove away and I never saw Harry Wright again," according to Coo as related to Slade.

Slade claimed that Harry Nabinger had returned home in time to see Wright's body on the lawn immediately after the accident. Rather than to be implicated, he left and was not found again until Eva and her friends picked him up near midnight, in Oneonta.

Now, marrying the Coo and Warner stories, Slade said that Mrs. Warner had begged Martha to tell the truth but she refused, still not believing that she was the victim of a hoax.

"Of course we know that isn't true," Slade told the Governor, "but who was the imposter; who was it that was taken to her and impersonated you?"

"Martha Clift in Bedford refuses to tell the truth. She refuses to tell the truth because she believes she will be freed as soon as Mrs. Coo is executed."

"Call Martha Clift here and question her. Get her to tell the truth and prevent this great miscarriage of justice."

Would the Governor, who was not famiilar with the case, accept the new script, long on imagination, distortion and drama, but short on logic? Grant, on the other hand, had already twice prevailed with his story so he again presented his history of the case as documented during the trial.

In addressing the contention that Eva should have testified, he remarked that Coo didn't go to the stand "simply because her lawyers knew if she did, the state would burst the case wide open. Eva didn't dare go on the stand."

In conclusion he said, "There is no personal satisfaction in sending this woman to the chair (but) is Eva Coo's life more precious than that of Harry Wright?"

On June 20, Warden Lawes also went to Albany. A reporter asked, "You are trying to get a commutation of Eva's sentence?"

"Yes," he replied.

Because the Governor was busy in another conference, Lawes laid his case before Charles Poletti, the Governor's counsel. While it was customary for Lawes to supply facts concerning condemned prisoners, it was rare indeed for him to make a recommendation. In fact, it had never happened before!! Was Coo's case the most flagrant miscarriage of justice he had ever witnessed or was he still smarting from Mitchell's stinging letter?

On June 26, affidavits were presented by Grant, Mitchell, Brady, and Tennant. Grant swore that he never saw Clift in jail; their meetings were always in the courtroom. The others swore that at no time had they visited her alone and that it would have been impossible for anyone to have impersonated the Governor within the jail.

IT'S OVER

While there seemed little chance that the Governor would buy Slade's tall story, Lawes had considerable prestige at the capital and it was bolstered by the fact that this was the first time he had interceded in behalf of one of his charges. It was still possible that residents of Ossining might be spared the dimming of lights within their homes as the system was taxed beyond its capacity during the moment that a surge of electricity raced through the body of yet another of Sing Sing's victims. Reprieves, when given, customarily came only moments before the prisoners were assisted through "the green door" that led to the stuffy room which served as the dreaded death chamber.

During the interim, prisoners could endure hell on earth more cruel than anything the devil might have in store for them in eternity. As Coo commented, "The worry and suspense is almost unbearable." Yet unlike those inmates who in the past had broken to the point of insanity, there was still some of the old Eva's strength and optimism. "It heartens me to know that Governor Lehman is still considering my request; I still feel he will do something for me. I suppose I'll go to Bedford, too," she confided to one of the matrons.

Coo had fierce and constant headaches, her days and nights one long nightmare. In a vain effort to alleviate the constant pain, the matrons kept changing the towels, dipped in ice water, that were wrapped around her head. She could not sleep. Seldom could she eat.

She still could not understand the provision in the law that all principals in a felony are equally guilty, regardless of the individual act of each. She believed that because she was not behind the wheel of the car that crushed out the life of Harry Wright, she should not be held responsible.

Furthermore, even if she were equally responsible, she was haunted by the discrimination against her. "I can't understand why anybody would wish me to go to the chair and the other one go to Bedford," she cried.

While she still showed little resentment toward the friends who had betrayed her, her love affair with Otsego County was definitely at an end. She told the warden that if she must die, it was her wish that her body be buried anywhere except beneath the stone that carried her name along with that of Harry Wright . . . the tomb that overlooked Portlandville.

It was clear that her remains would never return to the quiet countryside where as a child she had romped in the fields near Haliburton, Ontario. While her sister, Mrs. William A. Baker, as well as her aged mother had kept in touch with the authorities, none of her family had visited her or made plans to claim her body. In case they should arrive to bid her a last farewell, Eva had left instructions with prison officials that "I don't want them to see me in this condition."

Lawes professed more bitterness than Coo and he took one last pot shot. After commenting that she had received "a raw deal," he told Dorothy Kilgallen, "Her trial attorneys—do you know what they did to help her lately? Know what? One of them wrote me saying he'd like four invitations to her execution." Clearly he was not referring to to his proteges, the Slade boys, although they too had not done much for her lately.

According to the law, both District Attorney Grant and Sheriff Mitchell were required to recieve invitations to the execution. Both declined.

June 27, 1935 marked one year and thirteen days after the death of Harry Wright. That morning the sun climbed above the horizon while birds welcomed the dawn with songs of joy. Men and woman reluctantly climbed out of bed, grumbled over a cup of coffee, then went about their every day tasks. Life is fragile and some would never see another day, but ignorant of that fact, they would not savor those last few moments. This was not so in two of Sing Sing's cells.

In one sat Leonard Scarnici, a twenty-nine-year-old swaggering gangster, doomed to death on this day for killing a detective, but who bragged of "wiping out" twenty people during his career as a bank robber and gunman in quest of easy money. While playing pinnocle with a prison guard several days earlier, he had added the names of a couple more—two young fellows who he had recruited to help him during a robbery and then "bumped off" after the job was completed so that he could keep all the loot.

Scarnici had received three reprieves in the past, not because of any question of his guilt but rather in hopes that he might implicate some of his associates. He had played games with the justice system, holding out the possibility without any intention of actually betraying his friends.

In shackles, he had recently traveled to New York to appear in court. Enroute, he had remarked about the beauty of the sky, the fragrance of the fields, the music of the city streets, the exhiliration of the air he breathed— things he had never noticed in the past. Given the opportunity to trade his life for that of another, the criminals' code would have vanished but there would be no such opportunity. The best he could hope for was to have his fate postponed; he had run out of reprieves. He was resigned to die on this day.

In another cell sat Eva Coo who had conspired to speed up the death of her ailing handyman in order to supplement her failing income. Anyone who spends a lifetime on the razor's edge between respectability and crime is bound to eventually slip one way or the other. Eva had fallen on the dark side. Never again could she expect to pick berries on the Crumhorn or share a freshly baked cake with her neighbors during the day. Never again would she sing a bawdy song or serve drinks and banter to an appreciative, if boisterous, crowd during the evening.

She had gone through a terrible ordeal. Every time she had been offered a helping hand it had been used to push her closer to the chair rather than help her escape it. To the state, her life was useless; she had nothing to offer in exchange for a reprieve. Only a miracle could prolong her life another day and she knew it.

" . . . THE PIPER PAID"

During the afternoon, a small crowd of the morbid curious gathered outside the single front gate of the grim institution. There was a doubling of the guards, who stopped all cars before they could reach the parking lot.

"Execution night is always hard at Sing Sing," one guard said. "The men must work overtime, and extra precautions are taken, as executions upset the hundreds of other prisoners."

Thirty-four witnesses, physicians, guards, and newspaper men were beginning to arrive, there to watch as Eva's life was to be snuffed out. Should their eyes not be up to the task, their stomachs would not be spared as the faint yet sickening odor of searing flesh would permeate the room. Among the witnesses were two from Otsego County; Police Chief Frank Horton and the *Oneonta Daily Star's* city editor, A.M. Learned.

A pall hung over the prison entrance. "No commutation yet." There was a hopeful note in the guard's voice as he spoke of Eva's prospects.

Extra precautions had been taken to prevent a recurrence of the violation of prison rules when a photographer had snapped a picture of Ruth Snyder in the electric chair. In the warden's office, newsmen were warned that they were legal witnesses and must remain quiet in the execution chamber.

"Remember, no camera, boys," admonished the warden's secretary as he ushered them to the visiting room where they were searched expertly by three guards before embarking in the two "Black Marias" that took them the half mile to the deathhouse. Before entering the death chamber, they were again searched by three more guards. There was also a count taken to make sure it coincided with the number leaving the administration building.

Meanwhile, in the early afternoon, Lawes talked with Coo in his chambers. During their half-hour conversation, Eva again proclaimed her innocence. She said that she wanted to forgive everyone who had done her wrong and she hoped God would forgive her for any sins she might have committed.

Although offered any food she desired for her last meal, she chose only toast, on which she nibbled, and ice cream, which she ate sparingly. She found even a bit of tea hard to swallow.

After the back of her head was shaved, she was taken to a room adjoining the one within which she would soon meet her maker. There, a solemn group was assembled. They would soon participate in the ritual death march.

In the front, two matrons, Mrs. Carrie Stephens and Mrs. May Creighton were supported by a heavy-set guard who walked between them. Out of respect to Eva, Lawes had chosen the bulkiest matrons and largest guard on his staff to shield her from prying eyes as long as possible. Behind them, wearing a prison-made blue print dress, Eva walked, followed by Anthony W. Peterson, the chaplain.

By now the witnesses, newsmen and doctors had been ushered into the death chamber. Although brightly lighted, the tan walls, grey floor and church-like benches presented a morbid atmosphere in the stuffy room.

Although guards directed the file of observers to their seats in the order in which they entered the room, some refused to sit in the front row, barely more than an arm's length from the deadly chair. There was complete silence other than for the slight scribbling of pencils, as those present were awed by what they were about to observe.

In the center of the room, on a rubber mat, stood the grim chair. From its sides hung leather straps like tentacles of an octopus, ready to reach out and pluck its victim. The executioner busied himself by soaking the death cap in a pail of water.

The switch was scheduled to be pulled at 10:30 p.m. Lawes had not joined the witnesses, and with only three minutes of life remaining for Eva, he picked up his office phone and made one last plea for a reprieve. The governor's answer came in a single word. "No!"

By now the little squad was in the corridor. There, one of Eva's stockings was removed so that one leg would be bare. There were deep dark circles around her eyes, the result of hours of weeping. Yet now she had mustered an inner strength. She stood as straight and defiant as any solidier looking into the barrel of a firing squad's rifle. When she had first been incarcerated in Cooperstown she had vowed, "They ain't going to see me crying," and while during her solitude she could not hold back the tears, through shear determination she continued to deny her enemies the satisfaction of witnessing her despair.

Of the several first-hand accounts made by witnesses, A. Milton Learned desribed it best.

There was a whispered 'Here she comes,' and then dead silence reigned in the execution chamber as the firm tread of Eva Coo and her attendants were heard in the outside corridor.

The two matrons, visibly affected, and with a burly prison attendant between supporting them by the arm, entered first.

Eva Coo stepped through the `little green door' alone and unassisted, then stopped momentarily. She gave a quick glance about, the harried, defiant look of the hunted animal. The tigerish look was gone from her eyes, but in its stead was the appearance of a wounded deer, defiant to the end.

Her head was erect, her shoulders back, her arms straight at her sides, and her hands only half clenched, a handkerchief caught in one. She appeared well groomed, and her hair in particular looked well. She had asked that the front of it be saved, when the prison barber was preparing her for the chair, and her request was granted. From the side, the shaved portion at the back of the head resembled a shingle bob and did not noticeably mar her appearance. The hair had been newly cut, curled and bleached, and looked much better than during her trial in Cooperstown.

One quick, almost startled look about the roomful of silent, awed witnesses, and then with just the faintest hint of a sigh of resignation, she stepped forward firmly to her impending doom, the chair.

She sat down, and laid her head against the covered board headpiece. Startled at the lightning speed with which the five guards began to adjust the straps, she spoke in a hurried tone to the two matrons facing her, "Goodbye, darlings."

A muffled sound came as if she were trying to speak again as the blindfold and chin strap were quickly tied, leaving a middle portion of the face exposed.

It seemed only a split second, and the last guard was pulling at the strap around her chest. The leather creaked as he exerted force, and a muffled moan was heard.

She did not suffer long.

As the guard stepped back, it was the signal for the executioner, Robert Elliot, to pull down the switch which sent 3,000 volts coursing through her body from the death cap to the electrode against the right leg.

She strained against the straps, the leather creaked again, and her chest heaved despite the tight hold of the straps. Four times the executioner pulled down the switch, and four times the body strained in its bindings. There was a slight curl of smoke at the last.

Then a guard shielded her from view as the matrons, who had stood with closed eyes, shoulders shaking, turned away, and quickly left the room. The guard removed the bandages, wiped her face, mouth and chest with a towel, then stepped back for the physician to make his examination.

"I pronounce this woman dead," he said.

ASHES TO ASHES

In awed silence, the witnesses remained while Eva's body was transferred to a hospital bed and wheeled from the room. The matrons, still weeping, left the room, and the guards who had been in charge of strapping her to the chair stood with bowed heads and folded arms, almost in an attitude of prayer as though seeking divine forgiveness for the part they had played in one death and were about to play in another. The executioner resumed the task of soaking the death cap.

Then Scarnici strode in, a half smile on his sallow face. He took one last drag on his cigarette and after a guard pointed to the chair, he sat down. Quickly the straps were adjusted but before they were tight, he motioned for the warden who had by now joined the witnesses.

"All I want to say to those double-crossers up in Albany is that I'm a better man than they are."

Two minutes later he was declared dead.

The body of Scarnici, a mad dog killer, was claimed by his brother and shipped to Springfield, Massachusetts for burial. As for Eva, by mutual agreement she was not sent back to the hill country she had loved in her glory days. She had asked that her body not be returned to Otsego County and residents of that county had agreed that they didn't want her anymore now that she was dead than they had wanted her when she was alive.

Unclaimed by relatives, her body was taken in charge by the Mutual Welfare League, an organization of Sing Sing prisoners that was administered by prison officials. Under their direction, her charred body was buried near Adams Corners, Putnam County, the exact location—a potters field reserved for the unclaimed bodies of Ossining's Sing Sing prison inmates. As for her spirit, that too was buried or does the ghost of Otsego County's most famous outcast still roam free over the foothills of the Catskills?

Contrary to popular opinion, Eva Coo was neither the first nor the last woman to be electrocuted in New York State. The first was Mrs. Martha Place who died in 1899 for the murder of her stepdaughter; she also tried to kill her husband. Second was Mary Farmer in 1909, for murdering Mrs. Sarah Brennan with an axe in attempt to get the latter's money. Third, Ruth Snyder on January 12, 1928 who with her lover, Judd Gray, was electrocuted for the killing of Snyder's husband, and fourth, Mrs. Anna Antonio, who with Vincent Saetta and Samuel Faracci, was electrocuted in August 1934 for the murder of Antonio's husband.

Other New York State women executed before Eva by hanging were: Mrs. Margaret Houghtaling in 1817 for the murder of her baby. (A year later, another woman confessed on her death bed that she was the slayer of the child); Mrs. Elizabeth Van Valkenburg in 1846 for the poisoning of her husband; Mrs. Punkie of Utica in 1849 for the poisoning of her husband; Mrs. Anna Hoag in 1852 for poisoning her husband; and Mrs. Roxalina Druse in 1887 for shooting her husband.

For 73 years, the dreaded electric chair served as the public's revenge against people convicted of first degree murder in New York State. On August 15, 1963, Eddie Lee Mays, a smalltime New York City hood, had the dubious honor of being the last person to burn within it's tentacles. After the United States Supreme Court reinstated the death penalty in 1976, several states again adopted capital punishment in various forms. Under Governor George Pataki, New York rejoined their ranks in 1995.

Several states, by statute, electrocute murderers. In practice, through legal maneuvers and technicalities, most convicted murderers either eventually escape the chair or grow old before they are electrocuted.

Eva Coo had one short stay of execution and was dead in just over a year after her conviction. How the justice system has changed in just sixty years!

Eva Coo's treatment was harsh by 1935 standards. By today's standards, it was outrageous.

OBITUARIES

The effects of the Eva Coo affair did not stop with her death. There were a lot of loose ends to tie.

James J. Byard, Jr.:
Sunny Jim continued to practice law in Oneonta until he moved to Hartwick in September of 1939.

On Monday, January 19, 1942, he was to appear in Supreme Court in

Albany where he was to try a case before Justice Bergan. Byard did not drive, so he hired a taxi which was driven by thirty-three-year-old Frank Nugent of Cooperstown. Jim sat in the front seat next to the driver; his wife, Lulu, in the rear seat.

At ten a.m., as they neared the city, they were met by a westbound car driven by twenty-four-year-old Robert Dome of Cleveland, Ohio. Suddenly, as though thrust by the hand of an invisible power, the Dome vehicle went into a skid and crossed into the eastbound lane facing broadside to the taxi. The taxi struck the car head on and was demolished.

Dome was unhurt, Nugent suffered injuries to his head and knees while Lulu Byard sustained leg and head injuries that would hospitalize her for many weeks.

The missile may not have been a Willys Knight, but the injuries that it inflicted were practically identical with those that had taken the life of Harry Wright less than eight years earlier. With his rib cage crushed, severe lacerations to the face and a broken leg, he lay in Albany's St. Peters hospital. Even though unconscious, he valiantly fought one last battle—one which, like the Coo trial itself, he could not win.

Five days later, on January 24, 1942, he died. His body rests in what is now the "old" Fly Creek Cemetery.

Why James J. Byard Jr. took the Coo case is a mystery. It couldn't have been for financial reasons.He had large holdings of real estate, Coo had no money and the county paid a pittance.

He already had a reputation as the best criminal lawyer in Otsego and adjoining counties, and at the time he took the case, he had no way to know that the trial would place him in the limelight before a nationwide audience.

He knew Eva but there is no evidence that they were great friends. On the other hand, among his friends were people who wanted Eva quickly and permanently silenced. Yet, here again there is no evidence that he was party to a conspiracy. In fact, it is difficult to see how any attorney could have created a better defense with the evidence available.

Colleagues told Byard that he should not be surprised if he did not prevail in prejudiced Otsego County, but that he should have a good chance to get an aquittal upon appeal. Due to his error in judgement, that opportunity was denied him.

Yet, when Lawes stepped in to help Eva and discredit Byard, he handpicked the best attorneys he knew. Their major argument in a quest for a new trial was that Coo had not been adequately represented. The Court of Appeals dismissed that along with their other arguments. Slade & Slade, by in a sense putting Byard's expertise and dedication on trial, only proved that they could do no better for Eva and ironically they also established that Byard had given her competent and adequate counsel.

Perhaps it was pride.There is some evidence that Byard, the dean of regional lawyers, was not on good terms with the young rising star, Grant. (While descendants of Byard would not consent to an interview, a former county official familiar with the case described a brawl between the two attorneys when they met at a private home.)

While Byard had more experience in criminal law, he had never been the defense attorney in a murder case. Grant, as a prosecuter, had obtained convictions in two. Perhaps Jim saw the Coo case as a challenge . . . an opportunity to prove that he had superior talents.

Another enigma is why the blue-nose hypocrites who wanted to send Eva to her just rewards would allow the best barrister in the area to defend her— and as taxpayers, at their own expense. Perhaps it happened too quickly for them to prevent it but if, on the other hand, it was Christian charity, it is the only evidence of it in the Coo case.

Martha Clift:

Prison life was a living hell for Martha. While her letters never showed any remorse for snuffing out Harry's life, she was deeply saddened by the blight her indiscretions had inflicted on the lives of her mother and children.

Her mother, referred to as Anna in newspaper stories, and her stepfather, W.O. Miller, continued to care for her two offspring. In an effort to shield these innocent victims from their mother's notoriety, they quickly moved to Mt. Vision, then to Glenfield, New York.

Mrs. Miller had been in failing health before the trial. Now she was a complete invalid. Martha was ready to settle down and care for her mother and children. She, as well as other family members, pointed this out to Tennant, the parole board, and the governor but all to no avail.

On August 24, 1942, the parole board recommended to Tennant that Clift, upon her release, should not return to Oneonta and furthermore she should change her first name. Because her children had continued to use the name Clift, apparently their reasoning was that by changing her given name, she could carry the same maternal surname while not drawing attention to her colored past. This suggestion seems premature inasmuch as they then denied her parole.

Again on June 21, 1944, Governor Dewey denied Tennant's request that Clift be allowed to return to her family. In fact, the reformed Martha was not paroled from prison until November 11, 1947. She was discharged from parole on February 7, 1961. Martha's values had changed a great deal during those thirteen solitary years. The world had changed even more during her absence.

Rip Van Winkle slept twenty years and was astonished to see the changes that had taken place within that period. Yet they were small indeed when compared to the social and economic metamorphoses that had occurred during the thirteen years that Martha lived within prison walls. She entered during the depth of the Great Depression and emerged during the unprecedented post-war prosperity.

The reformed Martha quickly joined her family. While her children had retained the Clift name, she now used her maiden name, Martha Compton.

By now, her family had moved several times so she was able to join them some distance from the area in which her exploits were well known. What's more, newspapers no longer featured stories about the incident that had blighted her life. Incredibly, it was possible to keep secret the indiscretions of her youth from her neighbors and grandchildren all during the rest of her lifetime.

She led a quiet, simple life and is remembered by a grandson as "having a heart of gold beneath a tough exterior." However, he also noted a couple of idiosyncrasies which could only be explained after her adventures with Eva were revealed. (1) She never bought a car and would not drive if there were any possible way to avoid it. (2) She disliked journalist Dorothy Kilgallen who was by then appearing on the TV Show, "What's My Line."

During this period of her life, Martha never remarried. With her brother, Lester, and a sister-in-law, Rose, she spent many years as a caretaker, cook and maintenance person at a private hunting and fishing club on the Salmon River Reservoir north of Pulaski. After developing cancer, she lived awhile with a grandson. On June 24, 1983, her complicated and contradictory life came to an end at St. Joseph's Hospital in Syracuse. Her body rests in peace in the Richland, New York cemetery.

Eva Coo:

Sociologists can have a field day and prove any of a dozen lessons from the Eva Coo saga. In the county from which she was banished, her name still receives nearly as much recognition as do the area's promoted and pampered favorite sons. Not only the people of her time but their children, their grand-children, and great grandchildren have heard her legend repeated countless times—so often in fact that the legend has often wandered from the path of truth. Yet when one goes back to discover the truth, what is found is even more startling than the myths.

Donald H. Grant:

While in the limelight as prosecuting attorney, the newspapers frequently referred to Don Grant as being of "gubernatorial timber." While he never gained that high honor, he certainly continued a distinguished career. Even though he, above all the rest, seem to have taunted fate, Eva's curse missed it's mark.

In 1937 he was elected Otsego County Judge. On July 17, 1942, he re-signed this position to enter the military service as an infantry lieutenant. Serving with the 26th Infantry, 1st Division, he was wounded and gassed in action and was awarded the Silver Star with Oak Leaf Clusters, the Distin-guished Service Cross, and the New York State Distinguished Conduct Cross with two citations.

Following his discharge, he was appointed Otsego County Attorney and held that position for eighteen months. Governor Thomas E. Dewey ap-pointed him to the New York State Board of Parole, a position he held from July 1, 1947 to April 1, 1954.

After that, he engaged in the private practice of law until, in failing health, he retired in 1962. He died on Oct. 21, 1964 at the age of seventy-three.

Edna Hanover:

Pretty little Edna Hanover had lived off of Eva's largess during the hard times. When she had no place to stay, Eva had given her room and board. Even when she was not living at the inn, she used it as a base from which she was able to meet and profit from its patrons.

At the trial she maintained a flippant, devil-may-care attitude. She flirted with not only her captive audience, but through her damaging testi-mony, her benefactor's life.

Now the trial was over and she still was sponging off of Eva. After read-ing the articles in the *New York Sunday Mirror* . . . the same ones that were to haunt Byard for the rest of his life . . . she felt that her reputation had been damaged and that she had a case for libel. On January 12, 1935, a summons was served on the *Mirror*.

Rather than send their high-priced legal staff up into the wilderness to answer charges, the *Mirror* felt it would be less expensive to settle with her. The two parties agreed that her reputation was worth slightly over $500.

Before her death, Eva heard about Edna's payoff. Within a long letter written on May 6, 1935 to a friend, Mrs. Elmer Bastedo, she mentioned, "I see Edna got five hundred over that story and you would well imagine what I would get if I was out of here. She got that for them using her name. They didn't hurt her any. . . ."

At about the same time, Edna received a check from the county, compensation for the testimony she had given against Eva at the trial. With this money, stained with Eva's blood, she was able to turn in her battered old Ford for a shiny new Chevrolet roadster.

It was between 10:00 and 10:30 p.m. on October 25, 1935 that this sporty vehicle was speeding up the new highway between Unadilla and Wells Bridge. At the wheel, her head high and the wind blowing through her hair, was Edna Hanover and beside her, Theodore Kennedy, her date for the evening. In the back seat sat another couple. The party had concluded a wild night on the town and now was headed for an encore in Oneonta.

To the raucous music from the car radio, they sped up the winding road, exhilirated by the refreshments they had consumed and the car's speed

Was it a pat on the knee, a giggling response, a moment of distraction just as the road changed its course that brought a fast life to a fast finale? Or could it be that suddenly the headlights picked up the misty image of a friend from the past . . . an apparition that beckoned to her destruction? We shall never know.

Whatever the cause, two mangled bodies lay within a tangle of twisted steel. Like the cover of Harry Wright's coffin, the overturned vehicle pinned them in the rubble. Blood painted the highway and leached into the soil.

Cars began to stop so that passengers could view the carnage, but not until fifteen able bodied men had assembled, were there enough present to lift the vehicle off the victims below.

The couple in the backseat had been thrown clear of the vehicle. They had only superficial injuries but Theodore Kennedy, ironically a native of Carlton County, Ontario, not far from Coo's birthplace, was dead at the scene. Edna managed to hang on to her young life long enough to reach the hospital in Sidney; her death was recorded at five o'clock the next morning.

Dr. Norman Getman, the same coroner who had given a report of "crushed chest and internal injuries" in his report on the cause of death for Harry Wright was able to use exactly the same words for Edna's demise.

Eva Coo had been under the sod for over three months, but was she still up to her old tricks from her grave?

Dorothy Kilgallen:

Dorothy Mae Kilgallen was born in Chicago on July 2, 1913. In 1931, while still less than eighteen years of age, she followed in her father's footsteps by becoming a Hearst publications reporter. Like all cub reporters, at first she covered mundane functions such as social events and political meetings. Her talent for uncovering facts and reporting them in words so graphic that they appeared sensational while remaining a bit short of fiction, was soon recognized by her superiors. With no major wars in progress, the public was fascinated by stories of crime, and by 1934 she was covering the juiciest crime assignments including the Eva Coo murder.

A quiet evening could become an exciting adventure in the eyes of Dorothy Kilgallen. As an example, here are selected paragraphs from the story in the *New York Journal American* after she spent a night "alone" at the murder scene.

> I sat on the broken steps of the haunted Scott homestead, the boards moaning and moving beneath me, and if I turned my head I looked up at (a) bleak blackened caricature of a house standing alone there on the mountain leaning against the wind—its windows broken, its doors boarded like a mouth that has been gagged against talking.
>
> An owl cried to the yellow moon. A thing with wings hit against my shoulder. This must be a bat I thought. I moved inside the 'woodshed' part of the house, where they brought Harry Wright's dead body to show Eva after they had it out of the grave.
>
> From twilight, the hours they say Eva Coo came up these craggy slopes to kill for gold, until dawn, when the mountain pulled its head out of the swathing mists—I stayed. The silence and the blackness kept me awake. And I saw the ghost.

The story is typically Kilgallen, typically what the public demanded, and typically what sold newspapers for Hearst. It's not surprising that she was now getting the best assignments and becoming the foremost woman reporter of her time. From 1934 to 1965 she covered many of the sensational murder trials that once shocked and fascinated the American public. In addition, she became an influential Broadway columnist as well as a radio and TV personality known to millions for her participation in the "Dorothy and Dick" and "What's My Line?" shows.

Dorothy Kilgallen died in the early hours of November 8, 1965. The death certificate indicated the cause as a combination of alcohol and barbiturates; some believed there was foul play involved, but this was never proven.

Kenneth Knapp:

Trooper Kenneth Knapp played an important part in four murder investigations, the first of which was the Eva Coo case. By 1945 he was working out of the Delhi substation.

On July 17 of that year, in response to a call received at 2:50 p.m., he was sent to the Mills residence in the town of Colchester where an alcohol accelerated domestic dispute between thirty-nine-year-old Ernest Mills and his estranged wife, Dorothy, was in progress.

Looking in the window, he saw what he thought was Mill's body lying on the living room floor at the front of the house. Knapp entered through the unlocked back door and passed through the kitchen and dining room. As he moved into the living room, he was met by the blast of a 16-guage shotgun fired at point blank range. He died instantly.

Mills immediately fled to and barricaded himself inside his sister's house which was next door. Neighbors notified the trooper barracks and soon thirty state police armed with tear gas, floodlights and rifles, surrounded the dwelling.

Mills held the police at bay by threatening to shoot the building's three residents, who he was now holding hostage. In response to his shouted demands, Jackie, his ten-year-old son by a former marriage, was brought to the scene and the two talked to each other.

Shortly after eight p.m., several troopers rushed the house. As they were breaking down the door, they heard Mills shout, "Goodbye, Jackie," followed by a single shot from the same gun that had taken Knapp's life. Mills, like Knapp, died instantly.

A.M. Learned:

After graduating from Middlebury College in Vermont, Albert M. Learned became a reporter for the *Daily Republican* in his native town of Plattsburgh, New York in 1928. At age twenty-one, he became city editor of the *Franklin Daily Times* in Malone before joining the *Oneonta Daily Star* in 1932.

The *Star* was one of the smallest newspapers to report the events that took place during the murder, trial, and aftermath. Yet, as editor, Learned demanded and obtained the most accurate and responsible reporting as borne out by comparing trial transcripts with newspaper accounts. It also was his article (attributed to Sheriff Mitchell) in *True Detective Mysteries* magazine that got the sheriff in hot water. Learned and Police Chief Horton were the only Otsego County residents to actually witness Eva's execution.

During World War II, Learned was sent overseas as a field director with the American Red Cross. Later, he worked as a war correspondent attached to General Douglas MacArthur's Pacific Theater of Operations.

After the war, he became managing editor of the Geneva, New York *Daily Times* and editor of the Schenectady *Union Star*. For five years he worked for the American Cancer Society in Brooklyn before returning to Geneva to become director of the news bureau at Hobart and William Smith College. He retired in 1973 and died on July 1, 1993 in Geneva, New York at the age of 85.

George Mitchell:

The frivolous charges which were brought against George Mitchell on February 28, 1935 appeared to have little if any substance. What's more, the sheriff and the governor were of the same political party. Even so, Mitchell couldn't be complacent—he couldn't be sure whether the outcome would be decided on merit or the warm relationship between those who instituted the charges and those who would decide the outcome.

He was left in suspense until August 10, 1935. On that date, the governor sent him a copy of the letter he was mailing to Slade & Slade in which he said

> I have carefully considered your complaint against Mr. George H. Mitchell, Sheriff of the County of Otsego, because of the article pub-lished in the March issue of *True Detective Mysteries*, apportaining to the Eva Coo case.
>
> A copy of your complaint was submitted to the Sheriff and he has filed with me a verified answer, which I have considered.
>
> In my opinion, there is no further need for executive action in the matter.
>
> Very truly,
> Herbert H. Lehman.

After the end of his term, Mitchell returned to the family business. He ran for sheriff again in 1942 but this time he was defeated. He was 72 years of age when, in 1958, he died of a heart attck.

Harry Nabinger:

Harry had played a leading roll during the trial. Now that it was over, the adrenaline that had sustained him so well during this trying time had departed; the letdown had set in.

While there was no direct communication between them, in writing to her remaining friends, Eva had expressed her love as well as her concern for Harry's future. Harry, on the other hand, expressed no love, only compassion for Eva.

By now, everyone in Otsego County had heard of Harry Nabinger. The few people who had been rooting for Eva looked upon him as her betrayer; those who hated her, looked upon him as her friend and lover. It was a no win situation.

Harry's dependence on alcohol was no greater than that of some of the untouchables who were persecuting him. Yet, while their indiscretions would be overlooked, Harry's name was soon to appear again in the local papers. This time it was another stay in the county jail for drunken driving.

If Harry were to put his life back together again, it could never happen where he would always be faced with the ghosts of good times past. Neither was there any future in an area dominated by self righteous people who wanted to cleanse their domicile by banishing any remembrance of and any associate of the county's embarrassment.

Harry soon retreated to Binghamton where he had been raised and where many family members still lived. There he again found employment as a salesman. In later years he moved back to Detroit to be near his children. It was there where his turbulent and troubled life ended and where he found peace at last.

Harry Wright:

Harry Wright's body lies a-mold'ring in the grave—but that's about as far as one can parphrase the old Civil War ballad because no one seems to have cared. Neither Eva nor Martha ever indicated even the slightest regret for being repsonsible. Some of the "sob sisters" who covered the trial for the newspapers shed adjectives of sorrow for poor, persecuted Eva, but they totally forgot Harry.

Harry's tombstone sits at the top of the hill in the cemetery overlooking

Goodyear Lake. Only recently have the encroaching weeds and brush been cut to reveal that the stone now has his correct date of birth and Eva Coo's name has disappeared. Just as Harry's body has been buried three times and ressurected twice, so has the stone been lettered on three occasions and had letters removed twice—and yet no one can be found who has any idea of the history of the final inscription. However, there is a strong clue tucked away in the Surrogates office in Cooperstown.

On March 4, 1936, Mrs. Rosena M. Simmons, a cousin of Harry Wright, appeared with her attorney, W.I. Bolton, asking that Harry's will be declared null and void. Coo had been both the executrix and beneficiary. At stake were the twenty life insurance policies placed with eleven different insurance companies, all on the life of Harry Wright.

E.R. Campbell, who had drawn up the will was now Honorable E.R. Campbell, a Surrogate Judge, so he was automatically disqualified from presiding at the hearing. Judge Lee D. Van Woert heard the case on March 16.

He concluded that "I think there is an inescapable conclusion that Harry Wright, the maker of this alleged will, was influenced by this calculating woman, which is a notorious fact in this community and a well established fact before the court. The will antedates the murder only a few weeks, and the circumstances of Harry Wright's death are well known; he died at the hands of the beneficiary of this will, who took him to a law office for the purpose of having that will drawn. All the outstanding circumstances point only to the coercion and influence in the operation of a stronger mind upon a weaker one. I think the prayer of this petition should be granted and I declare that the will is null and void."

Mrs. Simmons was appointed administrix and claims were presented to each of the insurance companies involved. Under terms of the policies they could be contested for fraud or a variety of other reasons for a period of time after they were issued—as little as one year on some, as much as three years on others.

Of the twenty policies involved, only one of the three issued by Prudential had been held over three years so it could not be protested. It paid $980.20. Metropolitan returned $51.41, the premiums received on their three policies and Postal Life & Casualty returned the $7 premium they had received on one of their two policies. The other companies either refused outright or failed to reply. One company had itself died and was going through liquidation.

The $1,038.61 received from these proceeds were the only assets and after expenses of $732.58 were deducted, $306.03 was left for Harry's first cousins, most of whom he had never seen. Since there were fourteen cousins or their heirs, by the time the money was divided among them, each received only a small amount.

Perhaps Harry was the big winner. Hidden in the expense column is an item, "Dauley & Wright - lettering monument - $15." Obviously that was to return his birthdate to 1880 and remove Eva's name from the stone.

Harry Zindle:

Harry Zindle was the accidental hero in the Eva Coo case. It was he who accidentally observed intruders at the Scott house on Decoration Day. It was he who sent the Hunts and Finks to investigate. The timing again was such that they accidentally arrived at the precise moment that Coo and Clift were exiting the premises with Wright's body. A conviction would have been difficult if not impossible without this evidence, all of which was set in motion by Harry Zindle.

There is a paradox at every turn of events in the Coo case so it should not be surprising that Harry Zindle was one of the people most responsible for Eva's conviction. Yet he and his wife appeared as witnesses for the defense!!

Some accounts put Harry Zindle in the company of Harry Nabinger and Dorothy Kilgallen at the wake observed at Noble's Roadhouse on the evening of June 27, 1935. Be that as it may, it was less than two months later when he too, at the age of 58, would be in his grave.

A daughter remembers that on the evening of August 19 he had severe intestinal pains. One of his children ran barefooted down the gravel road to the nearest neighbor's house to summon help. The neighbor phoned for a doctor but none arrived. Harry died about one a.m. on August 20, 1935. There was no autopsy and he was buried in Plains Cemetery in Oneonta. The children were immediately put into foster homes.

Many rural New York residents lived in what we would now consider utter poverty during the depression. Yet most had an old car, horse or mule for transportation. The majority had electricity, a phone, a radio and the children owned shoes. Harry, his wife and children lived in a very remote area with none of these niceties. In spite of, or perhaps because of this humble beginning, Harry's family went on to become responsible, useful and successful citizens.

One of Harry's daughters told about how the Zindle children, as well as some others who lived on the Crumborn, attended Sunday School. A lady

would drive up the mountain every Sunday, dress them in suitable clothing
and take them to a service in a private home. She remembers how her father
would vigorously rub pennies on the carpet so that each child could give one
that would be bright and shiny when it came time to take up the collection.

Woodbine Inn:

In a deed dated August 14, 1928, Charles Hamm had originally sold
Woodbine Inn to Eva Coo. In a deed dated June 27, 1934, Coo was forced to
"sell" it báck to Hamm. However, by now the transaction, in addition to the
land and buildings, also included "all the personal property in said house
including the refrigerator, silver, dishes, culinary equipment, beds, table-
cloths, napkins and all other personal property on said place contained."

Byard and Hinterminster signed the agreement. It's doubtful that Eva
even received the traditional dollar that constitutes compensation on a sale.

An effort was made to resurrect it as a gathering place where the public
could "eat, drink, and be merry." It failed. In the past, Eva had called it
Woodbine Inn but her clicnts had called it "Eva's Place" and Eva was gone.
Without her, the charm too was absent.

Charles Hamm died and on July 27, 1943 the executor of his will
sold it to Agnes Wendler. She and succeeding owners lived there but made
few repairs. In 1948 (the deed is recorded December 7, 1950) William Van-
der Meullen purchased it and in a newspaper item dated May 13, 1953, he
proposed tearing down the decaying structure and constructing a two-story
combination residence, office and restaurant directly in back of the demolished building. While that never happened, a succession of people have purchased the land and built on it. However, Woodbine Inn, like the Scott hauted
house on Crumhorn and the matron who made both famous, has fallen into
decay.

THE INNOCENTS

Some people feel that Eva and Martha received more than just punishment, and some like to blame the reporters who descended on an unsophisticated rural area for corrupting the citizenry even though they "brought it on
themselves."

Our compassion might better be reserved for the anonymous victims,
many children, who had absolutely no control or responsibility for the life-

time of hell thrust upon them as the result of the irresponsible acts of others. To name them here would only serve to prolong their agony and yet they were the only martyrs in this tale of woe and should be recognized. The following story illustrates the point and is repeated with the permission of one of Martha's nephews.

It was during the depression and he was a youngster living with his father who was an itinerant workman, frequently moving from place to place. They were living in various parts of Otsego County in 1934 and, even though well underage, the son often accompanied his father into speakeasies, including Eva's place.

The father, Dick Compton, was Martha's brother and very protective of her well-being. Immediately after Wright was murdered, the son woke up one morning to find that his father was missing. He had left without even leaving a note. Needless to say, the boy was very upset and bitter, believing he had been abandoned. After being put in a foster home, he became even more disturbed; he hoped never to see his father again.

It was thirty years before a friend told him the truth and father and son were reunited. The truth was that Dick had known that Eva and Martha were planning to murder Wright. In fact he had even been asked to participate in the act. Repeatedly he tried to persuade Martha to give up her part in the plot, and she repeatedly refused.

Once the deed was done, Dick feared that having known about and yet not reporting the plot, he might be considered an accessory. Even more, he feared that he might be called to testify against the sister he loved. As the interviewee's wife commented, "That murder ruined the life of both my husband and his dad."

They certainly were not the only ones. Many innocent victims suffered as much as Eva and Martha and for a lot longer period of time.

POSTMORTEM

Accounts written at the time of the events carry day-to-day, blow-by-blow news items of the events. In the matter of seeing the big picture, reporters found it difficult "to see the forest because of the trees." It is also more than likely that the more perceptive journalists were afraid to venture into the forest for fear of the powerful beasts that lurked there. Even so, at least one brave, non-resident journalist did refer to the arrest and trial as "smacking of Jersey justice."

Even now, old-timers say that powerful people wanted Eva silenced as quickly as possible. Yet their eyes drop and their talk stops when they are asked to name names or to speculate as to how much these people were able to infiltrate or influence the justice system. Without witnesses, we will have to depend on circumstantial evidence which in itself is enough to draw a conviction in the eyes of many observers.

Yet, an analysis of the facts creates as many questions as it supplies answers. Some of the questions may in fact come full circle and cast doubts on the first conclusion. As an example, let's examine a few of the more obvious reasons why one might expect that an appeal was warranted.

It was Clift's purchased testimony that drove the final nail into Eva's coffin. Yet several of her statements were contradictory or not borne out as being the truth according to other testimony. Let's talk about the mallet which the prosecution claimed dealt a stunning blow to Wright's head and which certainly created a telling blow to Coo's defense.

There were two mallets in the Scott house, one of which had belonged to Ben Fink and he saw it on the front room floor when he visited the place on or about May 20, according to his testimony. On Decoration Day, it was possible, yes probable that Eva removed that tool and placed it on the porch for future use.

In sworn testimony, Harry Zindle, a witness for the defense, claimed that after the Coo party left on Decoration Day, he picked it up and returned it to the house and left it on a washstand. He then secured the door from the inside with a 30-penny spike and checked to be sure that all other entrances were locked. Three days after the murder, Ben Fink, a witness for the prosecution, testified that he found the mallet on the washstand inside the building.

On June 14, the night of the murder, Mrs. Fink and Mrs. Hunt, according to their testimony, used Coo's flashlight to check the house and found all the entrances locked. So now we have four people saying that the mallet was secured behind locked doors both before and after Coo arrived on the night of the murder.

Yet Clift testified that on the night of the murder, Coo pushed open the front door with her knee and her head and disappeared inside the house. She then approached the car, carrying her hands folded across the front of her body and after Wright approached, she produced the mallet, hit him with it and pushed him in front of the moving vehicle's right front wheel.

Could Coo have broken down the door which was nailed shut from the inside, taken the mallet and after the dastardly deed was completed, returned it to the table inside, nailed the door shut and somehow exited through locked doors in the minute or so of time between when the murder was committed and the time when the Hunts and Finks arrived on the scene? No. Absolutely not!!

With the emphasis placed on Eva's only physical involvement in the murder, this inconsistency alone seems sufficient to warrant a new trial.

Martha also testified that Eva placed Harry's body in the car while she (Martha) was carrying on a solo conversation with the Hunts and Finks. To do that in close proximity to a crowd of suspicious onlookers might be possible but it's unlikely that Eva had that much gall and if it were true, why wouldn't the death car leave until after Ben Hunt and company left the scene?

Then there is the matter of illegal evidence. Judge Heath called it that and then said that even so, it could be introduced as evidence. Granted, times and values have changed but why would the judicial system dedicated to upholding the law say that evidence was illegal but legal, wrong but right? It's an outright contradiction.

Then there is the grizzly reenactment. Clift and Coo might have expected more humane treatment had they lived in the dark ages and been captured by barbarians. In the year 1934, things like that didn't happen in a civilized nation—except on Crumhorn Mountain.

Everything moved too fast and there were too many rights uprooted. Surely there was a conspiracy. Right? Before we become absolutely convinced of that, let's look at what followed.

Granted, Otsego County had some very wealthy, very influencial citizens and they had good reason to want Eva put away as quickly as possible. They were the proverbial big frogs and Otsego County was their small pool. How would they fare among the sharks when they moved into the big sea?

Warden Lawes, at the state level, commanded great respect and power. Whether because of his desire for justice or his desire to eradicate his upstart enemies, the fact remains that he went all out to have Coo's conviction reversed. His mouthpiece, the Slade boys, in talking to the press referred to Otsego County residents as "hillbillies." It is reasonable to believe that they echoed the contempt of most of the powers in New York City and Albany.

It seems incredible that hillbillies, even those on the most prominent peak, could prevail against the city slickers they had offended. Yet the fact remains that seven appeal court judges each said that there were no grounds for an appeal. In essence the state said that Eva received a fair trial in every respect.

That brings the merry-go-round back to square one. If they found no fault with the conduct in her Cooperstown trial, how can we make a case against those who conducted it or the powers that allegedly lurked in the backround? It is difficult to read the account without concluding that Eva was railroaded. Yet state officials concluded that it was all legal, proper, and unbiased without outside influence. Otsego County was found not guilty!!

Still not satisfied? Then one can argue that in 1935, the nation was in the depths of the Great Depression. Newspapers made frequent references as to the high cost of the initial Coo trial. There also was a different attitude toward crime and punishment. If a person was guilty, it was the duty of the system to convict him or her. Period.

Times were hard; money scarce; Eva guilty by a predominance of the evidence. Why subject the taxpayers to additional costs simply because she was the victim of improper procedure or even collusion? Could it be that seven appeal court judges bestowed on errant Otsego County depression era state aid? Not likely.

One can find evidence to advance many theories . . . and prove none.

But what of Eva's finale? There is no question there. Warden Lewis E. Lawes summed it up best when he appeared before the press and, after saying that Coo was "the bravest person—man or woman—" to die in the chair during his prison career, then added, "She was guilty as hell, probably, but she paid for any crime she committed and she got the rawest deal any human will ever get. No matter what she did to others, that didn't change what others did to her. They took her property, her automobile, her parrot and her dog, even the money from her life story. Only two people ever visited her, two women and one of them was wearing her clothing, every stitch and particle."

SOURCES

DOCUMENTS

Byard, James Jr., Papers at New York State Historical Association Library Special Collection, Cooperstown, N.Y.

Byard, James III, Papers at NYSHA Library Special Collection, Cooperstown, N.Y.

Coo's Canadian Prayer and Hymn Books, in the possession of Bob Riddell, Colliersville, N.Y.

Coo's Order of Execution, in the possession of Frank Getman, Oneonta, N.Y.

Death Certificate, Edna Hanover, Sidney, N.Y. Town Clerk

Death Certificate, Harry Wright, Computer printout, Schenevus Town Clerk

Death Certificate, Harry Zindle, Xerox copy, Milford Town Hall

Deeds, Delaware County Clerk's Office, Delhi, N.Y.

Deeds, Otsego County Clerk's Office, Cooperstown, N.Y.

Doctor Winsor's Coroner's Report on Wright's Death, in the possession of Beverly Graves, Oneonta, N.Y.

Inquest on Harry Wright's Death, Upper Susquehanna Valley Historical Association, Oneonta, N.Y.

Mitchell Papers, Sheriff George Mitchell's collection of letters, documents, artifacts and clippings, in the possession of Jack Mitchell, Cooperstown, N.Y.

Oneonta City Directories, Huntington Library, Oneonta, N.Y.

Probate of Harry Wright's Will, Otsego County Surrogate Court Office, Cooperstown, N.Y.

Summons served on the *New York Mirror* by Edna Hanover, Upper Susquehanna Valley Historical Association, Oneonta, N.Y.

Trial Exhibits (Wm. Warnken photographs) at NYSHA Library Special Collection (#17.1), Cooperstown, N.Y.

Trial Official Transcripts, Affidavits, Confessions, etc., Otsego County Clerk's Office, Cooperstown, N.Y.

BOOKS AND MAGAZINES

Diary of the New York Executioner. Book by Robert Elliott, Hartwick College Library, Oneonta, N.Y.

Human Detective Magazine, in the possession of Jack Mitchell, Cooperstown, N.Y.

Kilgallen, book by Lee Israel, 4-County Book System

Look for the Woman. Book by Jay Robert Nash, State University College Library, Buffalo, N.Y.

Moore, Ed, collection of books re. Oneonta, Coo, Crumhorn Mountain, etc., New York State Historical Association, Cooperstown, N.Y. and Huntington Library, Oneonta, N.Y.

Murder One. Book by Dorothy Kilgallen, Hartwick College Library, Oneonta, N.Y., and Milford Free Library, Milford, N.Y.

They Died in the Chair. Book by Wenzel Brown, in the possession of Marjorie Cahoon, Oneonta, N.Y.

True Detective Mysteries Magazine, in the possession of Gary Woodrow, Mary land, N.Y. and Jack Mitchell, Cooperstown, N.Y.

Women of Evil. Book by Wenzel Brown, in the possession of Lavonia Miller, Portlandville, N.Y.

NEWSPAPERS

The Albany Times Union

The Binghamton Press

The Freeman's Journal

The Glimmerglass

The New York American

The New York Daily Mirror

The New York Daily News

The New York Sunday Mirror. "Eva's Life Story." Clippings (Oct. 14, 21, 28, Nov. 4, 11, 18, 25, and Dec. 9, 1935, issues in the possession of Beverly Graves; Oneonta, N.Y.; single complete copies in the possession of Arlene Schmitt, Oneonta, N.Y., Walter Beach Jr., Milford, N.Y. and Pete Molinari, Oneonta, N.Y.

The Oneonta Daily Star

The Oneonta Daily Star, complete original newspapers, Upper Susquehanna Valley Historical Association, Oneonta, N.Y.

The Oneonta Herald, copies 6-21-34 through 7-4-35 from microfilm

The Otsego Farmer

(Newspaper clippings were obtained from the collections held by scores of different individuals and organization, too many to credit individually.)

OTHER SOURCES

Clift's Parole, Bedford Hills Prison for Women, Bedford Hills, N.Y.
Detailed layout of 25-33 Chestnut St. building c. 1927, Tony Nilo, Olney, Md.
Zindle's Souvenir Mallet, (original) in the possession of Morris Liedkie, Milford, N.Y.